Threats Posed by Ungulate Herbivory to Forest Structure and Plant Diversity in the Upper Great Lakes Region

With a Review of Methods to Assess those Threats

Natural Resource Report NPS/GLKN/NRR–2009/102

Donald M. Waller[1], Sarah Johnson[1], Rachel Collins[2], Evelyn Williams[1]

[1]Department of Botany
 University of Wisconsin – Madison
 430 Lincoln Drive
 Madison, WI 43706

[2]Biology Department
 Roanoke College
 221 College Lane
 Salem, VA 24153

April 2009

U.S. Department of the Interior
National Park Service
Natural Resource Program Center
Fort Collins, Colorado

The Natural Resource Publication series addresses natural resource topics that are of interest and applicability to a broad readership in the National Park Service and to others in the management of natural resources, including the scientific community, the public, and the NPS conservation and environmental constituencies. Manuscripts are peer-reviewed to ensure that the information is scientifically credible, technically accurate, appropriately written for the intended audience, and is designed and published in a professional manner.

Natural Resource Reports are the designated medium for disseminating high priority, current natural resource management information with managerial application. The series targets a general, diverse audience, and may contain NPS policy considerations or address sensitive issues of management applicability. Examples of the diverse array of reports published in this series include vital signs monitoring plans; monitoring protocols; "how to" resource management papers; proceedings of resource management workshops or conferences; annual reports of resource programs or divisions of the Natural Resource Program Center; resource action plans; fact sheets; and regularly-published newsletters.

Views, statements, findings, conclusions, recommendations and data in this report are solely those of the author(s) and do not necessarily reflect views and policies of the U.S. Department of the Interior, NPS. Mention of trade names or commercial products does not constitute endorsement or recommendation for use by the National Park Service.

This report is available from the Great Lakes Inventory & Monitoring Network website (http://science.nature.nps.gov/im/units/glkn/index.cfm) and the Natural Resource Publications Management website (http://www.nature.nps.gov/publications/NRPM).

Please cite this publication as:

Waller, D.M., S. Johnson, R. Collins, and E. Williams. 2009. Threats posed by ungulate herbivory to forest structure and plant diversity in the upper Great Lakes region with a review of methods to assess those threats. Natural Resource Report NPS/GLKN/NRR–2009/102. National Park Service, Fort Collins, Colorado.

NPS D-88, April 2009

Contents

Tables

Executive Summary

1. The **National Parks** of the Upper Great Lakes region serve as outstanding examples of natural landscapes, home to plant communities of special significance including late successional forests and wetlands. They provide habitat that sustains populations of wildlife including large mammals like deer, moose, and wolves. The landscapes of these Parks have also served as unique 'land laboratories' for understanding key ecological processes including succession, plant-animal and prey-predator interactions, and rare plant persistence.

2. Large **ungulates** like deer, elk, and moose are popular and physically impressive wildlife species in the Upper Great Lakes region. Their populations have recovered from very low densities in the 19th century. Resurgent deer populations, in particular, now pose a threat, however, to the natural landscapes that have supported their recovery. Deer and moose now act as "keystone herbivores" capable of radically curtailing tree regeneration and the abundance and diversity of forest understory plant communities.

3. Ungulates consume oak and hickory mast, seedlings, and woody browse from a wide array of **woody plants**. Several conifers including Canada yew, eastern hemlock, and northern white cedar are particularly hard hit by white-tailed deer, though many deciduous trees are also strongly affected including yellow birch, northern red oak, and other species. Moose heavily browse balsam fir as a preferred species. These impacts can be pronounced when seedlings are scarce or growth is slow (as in shade-adapted late-successional species), strongly affecting patterns of sapling recruitment and thus canopy species composition.

4. Ungulates also graze on a wide range of grasses, sedges, and forbs, particularly in late spring and summer when these foods make up the majority of their diet. Moderate to high deer densities are associated with substantial reductions in the survival, size, reproduction, and density of palatable species and corresponding increases in the density and cover of tolerant grasses and sedges. Their abilities to affect many species as well as forest structure and composition make them a 'keystone' herbivore.

5. Ungulate impacts depend not only on ungulate densities but also on context including the abundance of available favored plant species, the nature and rates of their growth, and the availability of alternative food sources. The complexity of these interactions makes it difficult to predict deer impacts simply from deer abundance, particularly as such abundance estimates typically pertain to broad areas whereas deer impacts are often local and heterogeneous.

6. Heavy deer herbivory has also been associated with the invasion and spread of weedy exotic plant species including garlic mustard, buckthorn, and honeysuckle, and possibly the spread of Eurasian earthworms.

7. Because ungulate impacts on understory composition, shrub diversity and abundance, and canopy composition and structure can be profound and long-lasting, monitoring is important both for anticipating such impacts and for tracking recovery from overbrowsing.

8. Ungulate impacts affect an increasing proportion of landscapes in the upper Midwest. This makes ungulate-free zones scarce and of increasing value for evaluating impacts and providing refuges for those plant species most affected by ungulate browsing. Fenced exclosures maintained to exclude deer (but not smaller mammals) for many years are of great value for the same reasons.

9. The number, diversity, complexity, and significance of ungulate effects make it important to **monitor** their impacts. Such monitoring can take many forms and can potentially provide early warning of impending substantial and difficult-to-reverse impacts. Because they employ similar sampling techniques, it is often efficient to incorporate ('piggy-back') monitoring of ungulate impacts onto routine vegetation surveys and monitoring.

10. Monitoring ungulate impacts on **woody plants** typically involves either directly tracking stature or the number of browsed twigs or indirect inferences of browsing based on demography (e.g., the relative proportions of individuals in various size or age classes). The former better characterize transient and recent impacts, while the latter provide a longer-term picture integrating over past ungulate impacts and potentially providing an 'early warning' indicator of impending regeneration failure.

11. Monitoring direct impacts of ungulates on **herbaceous species** typically includes tracking visible signs of browsing particularly on leaves, upper stems, and floral/fruit pedicels. Although indirect demographic techniques (e.g., size distributions or flowering percentages) can also be used to infer impacts on forbs, these techniques become ineffective once ungulate impacts are sustained or exceed a threshold where high herbivory causes palatable species to disappear or become too scarce to monitor.

12. It is often of particular value to monitor particular **indicator species** known to be palatable to ungulates including many rarer species (or age/size classes) of conservation concern when these are encountered. However, their rarity, particularly after browsing, makes it more difficult to obtain sample sizes large enough to provide adequate statistical power to reliably infer impacts.

13. Given these last two points, we have an incentive to develop **synthetic monitoring** techniques and methods of analysis that make use of data from several species. These can be based either on direct measures (e.g. levels of browsing on the woody plants present at a site) or indirect inference (like a community's overall species composition and/or patterns of relative abundance). Such pluralistic approaches add statistical power by taking advantage of all species and age/size classes present. However, we still lack a full understanding of how to construct these synthetic

measures and how their components respond to the transient short-term and longer-term impacts of ungulate browsing.

14. Fenced **exclosures** are of particular value for monitoring ungulate impacts for several reasons. a) They provide direct evidence of ungulate impacts in a controlled experimental setting. b) Such exclosures can be placed to evaluate ungulate impacts on particular species or in particular areas and to assess how these accumulate over time. c) They can provide visually arresting demonstrations of ungulate impacts with great educational value. However, exclosures can also inflate impressions of ungulate effects by creating extreme comparisons to an artificial zero-browsing baseline. To be most useful, exclosures should be replicated and maintained to allow detailed comparisons of community responses over time.

15. It is important to **sustain monitoring** programs to fully assess the short- and longer-term ecological impacts of ungulate browsing. While some populations and species appear resilient and quick to recover from ungulate browsing, other populations and species appear sensitive to browsing and slow to recover, particularly in fragmented habitats. As data accumulate over time, we gain better knowledge for evaluating how ungulate browsing affects particular plant species, the communities they occupy, and the conditions that favor their recovery. To be most useful, ungulate impact monitoring programs should include replicated exclosures, cover a range of deer densities and landscape conditions across space, and be sustained over time.

16. Monitoring ungulate impacts remains **a developing art**. Monitoring in the past has often been local and haphazard, focusing on only a few populations or species for a few years with a limited agenda. Future monitoring programs should be carefully designed, extensive in space and time, and subject to regular review and refinement.

17. The National Parks in the Lakes States have a **special opportunity** to design and implement a more comprehensive and sustained monitoring program on ungulate impacts. Such a program should incorporate a contemporary understanding of which relevant variables to monitor, adequate sampling to provide statistical power, and regular reviews to evaluate how the program might be modified to make it more efficient and effective.

18. There may be opportunities to **partner** with **state** and other **federal agencies** in the region to develop and implement such a comprehensive and sustained 'adaptive monitoring' program. Such monitoring would reap many rewards over the years including a fuller understanding of ungulate – plant community interactions and greater public support for ungulate management efforts.

Introduction

National Parks in the U.S. serve many roles. Since the 1960's, they have been managed to provide "vignettes of primitive America" to preserve and sustain native plant and animal diversity including large mammal ungulates and predators. That vision was first clearly laid out in the 1963 Leopold Report (by a committee of distinguished scientists chaired by A. Starker Leopold) which stated "As a primary goal, we would recommend that the biotic associations within each park be maintained, or where necessary recreated, as nearly as possible in the condition that prevailed when the area was first visited by the white man." While that goal can be criticized as impractical or unattainable, it did establish the importance of sustaining natural landscapes which clearly include in our region late-successional or old-growth forests as well as viable populations of large mammals and the natural processes that sustain these systems. It has gradually become clear, however, that populations of native large ungulates can grow to the point where they threaten the diversity and integrity of the forest that sustains them. This is particularly the case where native large predators are rare or absent and in situations where surrounding landscape and/or cultural conditions foster deer overabundance. It has become clear that "no park is an island" (Janzen 1983). This growth in ungulate populations has created a conflict wherein management to favor deer or moose (the only large mammals most visitors are likely to see) now threatens the persistence and viability of palatable plants, understory plant diversity, and even the regeneration of key late-successional tree species in many Parks. In light of this conflict, it behooves the Park Service to acquire adequate knowledge about these interactions and to use this knowledge to construct and sustain a monitoring program capable of providing accurate and reliable information about the nature, extent, and consequences of deer impacts on understory plants.

History, Scope, and Objectives of this Report

The National Park Service established the Inventory and Monitoring (I & M) program in 1996 to address public mandates being declared in response to a growing awareness of current and impending global ecosystem changes. Under this program, National Parks sharing ecological and physiographic characteristics have been organized into 32 networks in order to designate key indices, or 'Vital Signs', for monitoring ecosystem health across regional levels. The national I & M program has identified 46 Vital Signs linked to air and climate, geology and soils, water, biological integrity, human use, or ecosystem pattern and processes (Route and Elias 2005). Here in the upper Midwest, the Great Lakes I & M Network (GLKN) consists of 9 parks that are similar in being associated with major freshwater systems.

'Problem Species' such as white-tailed deer (*Odocoileus virginianus*) were identified by the GLKN as the fifth highest priority among the 46 Vital Signs (Route and Elias 2005). White-tailed deer are a native component of the Great Lakes region yet their increasing populations are negatively affecting native plant and animal populations and communities. In Wisconsin, deer population numbers have at least tripled since the inception of the Department of Natural Resource's (DNR) population modeling in 1960 (Wisconsin DNR 2005). Ironically, deer population numbers in the 1960s were already considerably higher than 25-years before when Aldo Leopold first voiced concerns about uncontrolled deer numbers (Leopold 1933, 1936, 1946). These impacts include inhibiting tree regeneration, reducing cover, and shifting the balance among plant species. His suggestion that we assess deer impacts via plant ecology research has now been addressed by numerous studies most of which have provided results that concur with Leopold's insight and intuition (see Miller et al. 1992; Waller and Alverson 1997; Rooney 2001; Rooney and Waller 2003; and Côté et al. 2004 for reviews).

Given the many impacts of ungulates on vegetation, wildlife, and other natural values (see below), there was a need to consider further the options available for monitoring ungulate impacts in the Great Lakes Region and how these might be integrated with the General Terrestrial Vegetation Monitoring Protocol (Sanders et al. 2008) that was initiated in Summer 2007. This Report was commissioned under contract with the NPS to review "The state of knowledge and future monitoring of white-tailed deer browsing impacts in the Great Lakes Network." It is intended to assist the GLKN regional ecologists in developing a Standard Operating Procedure (SOP) for surveying and monitoring deer impacts within vegetation monitoring plots throughout the nine National Parks in the region.

In this Report, we first briefly review what is known regarding deer impacts on forest ecosystems in the upper Midwest, emphasizing the historical trajectory of these concerns and recent knowledge. We then discuss the different approaches and methods that have been developed to monitor and interpret these direct and indirect impacts on both woody and non-woody plants. This will lead to discussions of the various kinds of data generated by different approaches to monitoring ungulate impacts and their relative value and statistical power. Finally, we synthesize these results and comparisons to develop recommendations for designing an efficient ungulate monitoring program capable of providing data of increasing value for evaluating ungulate impacts and managing wildlife populations so as to sustain plant diversity and other ecosystem values and services. Although "browsing" strictly applies to herbivory on woody stems and leaves, we use the term loosely in this Report to refer to herbivory on herbaceous plant parts as well.

We also conducted field work in conjunction with this project in the Apostle Islands and Pictured Rocks National Lakeshores (APIS and PIRO) in 2005 and 2006. This research was aimed first at assessing long-term changes in Apostle Island plant communities since the pioneering surveys of Ed Beals, Grant Cottam and Vogel in the late 1950's (Beals et al. 1960). Many ecologists now recognize the 'missing baseline' problem as severe, leading to a situation that John Magnuson (1990) terms the 'invisible present.' The extensive vegetation surveys of University of Wisconsin professor John Curtis and his students, however, have provided excellent baseline data for detecting and interpreting ecological change over the past half-century in Wisconsin (Leach and Givnish 1996; Rooney et al. 2004; Mudrak et al., in press). We also conducted studies at Pictured Rocks to compare alternative methods for assessing contemporary deer impacts on forest vegetation. We expect to present results from this latter project in a future paper.

This report draws on many sources including direct field observations, years of research into deer impacts by the authors, interviews with Park personnel, field work in the Apostle Islands and Pictured Rocks National Lakeshores (APIS and PIRO) in 2005 and 2006 (Mudrak et al. 2009 and forthcoming ms), and results from the many studies represented in the citations provided at the end of this report. Indiana Dunes NP was visited May 23-24, 2005, Apostle Islands from May 31 – June 1, 2005, and Pictured Rocks in July, 2005.

Parks as Laboratories for Understanding Ecological Processes

For many years, Parks in the Upper Great Lakes region have served as important field laboratories for researchers investigating a range of ecological processes. Early in the 20th century, Henry Cowles and George Clements did classic work on ecological succession on the dunes in northern Indiana that became the National Lakeshore. The studies by David Mech, Rolf Peterson, Peter Jordan, and others of moose, wolves, and forest dynamics on Isle Royale are world famous as well. The islands in Lakes Michigan and Superior are also famous as laboratories for investigating deer impacts on vegetation. This work includes classic work on the Manitou islands (now part of Sleeping Bear Dunes NL) and the Apostle Islands by Ed Beals and Grant Cottam (1960).

The Significance of Ungulate Browsing

After almost being exterminated from broad areas of the eastern and Midwestern U.S. in the 19th century, white-tailed deer made a remarkable comeback in the 20th century to become the region's most abundant large mammal. Bag limits, restricted hunting seasons, habitat improvement projects, and buck-only hunting were all embraced as methods to ensure recovery of the deer population. These efforts succeeded and white-tailed deer now exist across much of the eastern and Midwestern U.S. at record densities (probably aided by mild winters, favorable habitat conditions, and perhaps winter feeding). In northern Wisconsin deer are thought to have occurred at a density of 2–5 overwintering deer per square kilometer of suitable habitat before European settlement (McCabe and McCabe 1984). Densities now range from 8 to >20 deer per square kilometer through most this region (Garrott et al. 1993) and are even higher in southern Wisconsin. Total deer populations in Wisconsin, for example, increased from 600,000 in 1960 to more than 1,100,000 by 2000 (Wisconsin DNR 2005). Moose had a smaller-scale but in some ways analogous colonization and population growth on Isle Royale in Lake Superior in the 20th century.

These recoveries, however, have brought problems of their own in the forms of crop damage, vehicle accidents, outbreaks of disease, failed tree regeneration, and impacts on a wide array of understory plants and ecosystem processes. There are now widespread concerns over whether current high densities of deer are sustainable or compatible with maintaining natural values with a full complement of native species. On Isle Royale, there are concerns about whether the balsam fir forests   that dominated that island when deer arrived in the early 20th century will persist. Thus, conflicts are emerging between our region's flagship grazing and browsing mammals and the natural plant communities that sustain them. These conflicts have drawn increasing attention, e.g. in Pennsylvania (deCalesta 1994; deCalesta and Stout 1997; Frye 2008) where even a protected virgin forest has suffered severe declines in native plant diversity (Rooney and Dress 1997).

Although forest cover and dominance have been maintained across northern Wisconsin and the adjacent western Upper Peninsula of Michigan, this region also appears susceptible to ungulate impacts on forest plant community quality and diversity. In particular, resurveys of upland forests in the region reveal that local understory species richness has declined by nearly 20% over the past 50 years with sites also becoming more homogenous (Rooney et al. 2004). This forest homogenization is reflected in the general replacement of biotically-pollinated and dispersed native species by native graminoids, ferns and exotic species (Wiegmann and Waller 2006). The 'winning' species typically display traits that allow them to tolerate herbivory (i.e., plants with high fiber and low nutrition contents, low meristems, etc.), while less-tolerant species (i.e., those with palatable and nutritious leaves and conspicuous flowers and fruit) have declined. These non-random shifts in composition point to selective pressures on the system by white-tailed deer. Many other studies support this interpretation (e.g., Anderson 1994, Balgooyen and Waller 1995, Rooney 1997, Augustine and Frelich 1998, Augustine and McNaughton 1998, Webster et al. 2001). Impacts on groundlayer species in the Spring and Summer extend to the mid-story during winter. In the Great Lakes region, these effects are particularly dramatic on Canada yew (*Taxus canadensis*) stature and density (Frelich and Lorimer 1985; Allison 1990; Balgooyen and Waller 1995), eastern hemlock (*Tsuga canadensis* – Anderson and Loucks 1979; Frelich & Lorimer 1985; Rooney & Waller 1998; Woods 2000), and northern white cedar (*Thuja occidentalis* – Blewett 1976; Rooney et al. 2002). Parallel impacts have been documented in similar systems involving congener tree and ungulate species (Martin and Baltzinger 2002; Vila et al. 2003; Stroh et al. 2008).

Even the seemingly protected natural areas that have been placed into the protection of private or public agencies such as the National Park system are not immune to impacts on native species richness (Janzen 1983). In our study of long-term changes in understory species composition in Wisconsin forests, we observed particularly dramatic (>50%) reductions in plant diversity in two State Parks and generally lower richness in natural areas where hunting is restricted (Rooney et al. 2004, Rogers 2006). Resource managers of the National Parks within the Great Lakes Network have voiced concerns about the impacts of deer and moose (at Isle Royale National Park) on tree regeneration and native plant populations within park boundaries. We interviewed and surveyed park managers for this Report. Many cited anecdotal evidence of ungulate impacts including obvious browse lines on trees and shrubs, lower numbers of saplings and poor regeneration for certain tree species, and fewer broad-leaved wildflowers in the forests.

Many studies (Balgooyen & Waller 1995; Rooney et al. 2000, 2002; Rooney et al. 2004; Wiegmann & Waller 2006) identify deer herbivory as a major factor affecting understory plant abundance and long-term shifts in community composition in forests of the upper Midwest. We also observe changes in relative abundance and community composition that reveal responses of particular plant traits (primarily % fiber and energy content) to deer, as expected if these affect the nutritional value and palatability of plants to deer.

While other factors clearly affect long-term changes in these communities (including invasive exotic earthworms and shrubs and surrounding landscape conditions), impacts from deer alone and in combination with other factors remain a primary force in driving changes in Midwestern forest communities. This supports the notion that deer act as a 'keystone herbivore' in the region (Waller & Alverson 1997).

Top-Down Trophic Cascades

Ecologists have perennially been interested in learning whether predators have the ability to regulate population densities and/or the behavior of their prey and whether herbivores, in turn, have the ability to further regulate the abundance of the plants they consume. Such cascading effects on lower trophic levels could eventually act to limit plant abundance and primary productivity, as initially explored in aquatic systems (Carpenter et al. 1987). For many years, Caughley (1970; 1983) argued that A. Leopold and others had overstated the case that terrestrial predators could exert such 'top-down' effects on their ungulate prey in essays like "Thinking Like a Mountain" (Leopold 1949). More recently, however, evidence has again begun to accumulate supporting the notion that top-down effects may be important (Karr et al. 1992; Williams et al. 2004; Binkley et al. 2006). In western U.S. National Parks, Ripple and Beschta (2003, 2004a, b) have accumulated evidence that wolves reintroduced into Yellowstone NP are reducing the impacts of elk on vegetation, particularly along rivers. Such effects could reflect reductions in elk density, increases in elk movement and wariness (the 'ecology of fear'), or both.

Nelson and Mech (2006) found that wolf depredation had apparently long-lasting effects on deer in NE Minnesota at the northern edge of their range. With their populations supported by moose, wolf densities may have been great enough to prevent deer from recolonizing a 3000 km^2 region. Although wolves continue to keep moose wary on Isle Royale and may have acted to help curtail their population growth in the past, wolf populations in recent years appear fairly independent of moose dynamics. This is partly because wolves have declined in response to canine diseases (Brandner et al. 1990; McLaren & Peterson 1994) and perhaps also because moose populations are declining broadly across the region over the past 20 years, apparently in direct and indirect response to stress from warmer temperatures (including attacks from parasites spread by deer – Jones 2008). Researchers are now beginning to investigate possible cascading effects of wolves on deer in the region with some preliminary evidence that deer impacts may decline in cedar swamps near wolf pack territory centers (D. Anderson et al., in prep.).

Deer Diseases and Public and Wildlife Health Issues

Deer are now also associated with emerging diseases such as Chronic Wasting Disease (**CWD**) in S Wisconsin and N Illinois and **bovine tuberculosis** present in the NE lower peninsula of Michigan. Park managers have become concerned with these diseases not only because they may pose a threat to native ungulates but also because they could spread to other species and affect their power to manage wildlife populations. Sleeping Bear Dunes personnel, for example, express concerns about outbreaks of bovine tuberculosis in free-roaming deer in southern Michigan. The disease can be laterally spread to other warm-blooded fauna, potentially posing a threat to humans (Michigan DNR 2006). If southern Wisconsin populations of deer infected with CWD can not be contained, this prion disease could continue to spread and eventually reach most of the Parks in the region. While deer eventually die from this disease, mortality is usually delayed and far more males than females are infected. Thus, it fails to curtain deer population growth. Like bovine tuberculosis, its spread appears to be faster in areas where deer densities are high and over feeders or salt licks where deer may readily expose each other. In addition, there is the risk that white-tailed deer could spread diseases and parasites to other species of wildlife or humans. For example, CWD can be transmitted to elk, potentially a high risk for Voyageurs National Park if the disease is not contained. There is no evidence yet to suggest that CWD can transmit to humans, but hunters have been warned to not eat untested meat from the CWD zone in Wisconsin. Outward spread of the disease is also likely to reduce recreational hunting throughout the region, currently our primary means of deer herd management.

Many park managers also voice concerns about the increasing number of cases of **Lyme disease**, transmitted by deer ticks which may be growing in number as deer herds increase. For example, the number of reported Lyme disease cases in humans in SE Wisconsin tripled between 2007 to 2008 (600 to 1800 cases). Finally, deer are involved in 40,000 to 60,000 collisions with vehicles each year in both Wisconsin and Michigan representing a leading cause of accidents in many counties and more than 15% of the crashes in Wisconsin (Wisc DoT). Between 1979 and 2001, the Wisconsin DoT reports that number of injuries and deaths increased from 220 to 810 per year with the rate now remaining steady at about 36 per 100 million vehicle miles traveled.

Moose populations are crashing in NW Minnesota, from more than 4000 twenty years ago to fewer than 100 now (Jones 2008). Moose are near the southern edge of their range at Voyageurs NP. Resource managers are concerned that moose there are susceptible to **meningeal brain worms** that live as a heartworm in deer. If deer densities are high, they transmit these worms at a rate that can threaten the persistence of moose, elk, and other large ungulates. Whitlaw and Lancaster (1994) determined that North American moose populations are negatively impacted by meningeal worms when associated deer densities are greater than 5 per km^2. When elk were re-introduced to Wisconsin, they were particularly located in an area surrounded by wetlands near Clam Lake so as to isolate them from deer as a likely source of infection by these worms or other disease agents (L. Parker, pers. commun.).

Deer and Moose Impacts in Upper Lake States Parks
Park managers and NPS and USGS biologists are well aware of the impacts that white-tailed deer and moose have on vegetation in Parks in this region. In this section, we review the situations that exist in a few particular Parks, the perspectives of some Park managers and personnel there, and the knowledge bases and tools that exist locally to evaluate and respond to ungulate impacts. In this regard, we note that hunting is explicitly allowed under the original Park enabling legislation at Indiana Dunes, Sleeping Bear Dunes, Apostle Islands, and Pictured Rocks.

At **Apostle Islands** and **Sleeping Bear Dunes** National Lakeshores, deer have invaded islands that were historically not inhabited by deer. Also, deer are threatening to invade some of the Apostle Islands that currently maintain *no* deer populations. The Apostle Islands offer us an invaluable system for studying the influence of deer in that islands differ in their histories and intensities of deer occupation. Canada yew (*Taxus canadensis)* has received considerable attention on the Apostle Islands due to the exceptionally robust populations that exist on deer-free islands, and how quickly this evergreen shrub declines in abundance and vigor once islands are invaded by deer (Balgooyen and Waller 1995). Allison (1990a, b) determined not only that deer browsing reduces the density of yew, but also that deer interfere with sexual reproduction by initially consuming the male reproductive cones to the point that female cones are not fertilized and seed set declines. In a study on the 50-year changes in the composition of the groundlayer among forests across the archipelago, sites on islands that have never had deer are more similar to each other than sites that have been invaded by deer during the past 50-years (Mudrak et al. 2009). Indirect impacts of deer on plant height have also been noted among the Apostle Islands. For example, showy wildflowers such as blue-bead lily (*Clintonia borealis*) are larger on deer-free islands, suggesting that deer are selectively eating larger plants on islands with deer (Balgooyen and Waller 1995).

Of all the Parks in the region, **Indiana Dunes** National Lakeshore faces the highest deer densities and the most challenging management issues. These reflect both the fact that it has the highest plant species and habitat diversity in the region and the fact that it is surrounded closely by dense human settlements. These surrounding communities act both to boost deer populations (by providing habitats and, at least in the past, artificial feeding) and to restrict management alternatives. It is thus not surprising to find INDU most concerned with deer issues and most involved with evaluating the nature and extent of deer impacts and possible management strategies. The comments here stem largely from discussions with Park personnel including Randy Knutson and Noel Pavlovic.

Most INDU Park staff appear concerned with deer impacts and interested in taking steps to limit deer impacts. Although the Park lacks explicit historical data on local deer densities (and Indiana does not track these), the impression was that deer densities had been lower in the 1970's when snow storms may have limited their abundance. However, starting in the 1980's, milder winters and favorable landscape conditions favored growth in the deer herd leading to the current situation that most consider overpopulated. The eastern unit, in particular, appears to be losing plant species to deer herbivory though these effects are confounded with the impacts of fire suppression and nitrogen deposition (with unknown interactions among these factors). For example, direct deer trampling has apparently eliminated *Hudsonia* from some of the eastern dune barrens. These concerns have led staff to seek more data on deer densities and impacts and to construct exclosures.

Although we lack routine monitoring of deer densities in INDU, staff have encouraged research and collaborations with several scientists. These include spotlight surveys at night in February (Brian Underwood), three 20x20m 'large' exclosures built in the late 1990's (in collaboration with George Parker, Purdue U.), and the construction of many smaller (1 m²) exclosures immediately over known rare plant locations. In addition, nearby communities have paid for deer counts based on overflights with infrared imagery. Although not cheap, such data are valuable for being able to localize where deer are congregating as well as providing accurate population estimates. In addition, although they were not routinely monitoring deer impacts on vegetation in 2005, they do considerable vegetation monitoring data in association with their fire program and the experimental exclosures.

Indiana Dunes National Lakeshore personnel have done extensive research to refine survey methods and identify particular indicator species. Their list of 'Plants to be monitored and action thresholds" includes white baneberry (*Actaea pachypoda*), Pitcher's thistle (*Circium pitcheri,* a federally threatened species), *Trillium, Osmorhiza, Uvularia, Lupinus, Polygonatum biflorum* var. *commutatum* (observed heavy browsing after fires), jack-in-the-pulpit (*Arisaema triphyllum*), and *Maianthemum canadensis.* Field surveys on plant heights for three of these herbaceous plants, sweet cicely (*Osmorhiza claytonii*), jack-in-the-pulpit (*Arisaema triphyllum*), and white baneberry (*Actaea pachypoda*) provide evidence that these species could provide early detection of deer impacts on the groundlayer (Webster et al. 2001). Fletcher et al. (2001) identified the reproductive activity (% in fruit) of lily-look-alikes Solomon's seal (*Polygonatum* spp.) and False Solomon's Seal (*Maianthemum racemosum*) as sensitive indicators of deer impacts. Resource managers at Indiana Dunes have installed and are monitoring numerous exclosures to make comparisons of plant growth and reproduction of *Trillium* plants available to and protected from browsing deer. As is the case with the majority of the GLKN parks, tree seedlings and saplings, especially oak and cherry species, have also been identified as targets by browsing deer at Indiana Dunes.

In response to this knowledge and the concerns it has generated, INDU staff have started to try to get community support for lethal deer control efforts. They have also lobbied the state of Indiana for INDU to be declared a separate Deer Management Unit. State Parks in N Indiana have been hunting deer since 2000 using a special 2 day hunt that might serve as a model. Their plan would be to hunt continuously for 4 years to initially control the herd, then hunt every 2nd or 3rd year to sustain lower densities, basing management decisions on the success rates of hunters spaced out across the Park. Interestingly, the nearby communities of Dune Acres and Beverly Shores have now banned feeding and are resorting to hired sharpshooters to control excessive deer numbers.

Hunting is also the primary means of managing deer at **Apostle Islands** and **Pictured Rocks** National Lakeshores and the **St. Croix National Scenic Riverway**. Hunting is also effective at managing herds on South Manitou Island of **Sleeping Bear Dunes**, but coyotes have primarily been controlling deer numbers on North Manitou Island. Coyotes only began occupying the island in the 1980s; hence, resource managers have an additional level of complexity to consider. If deer numbers decline, then it is possible that the coyotes would in turn begin impacting native populations of hares, rodents, reptiles, and foxes on the island. Alternatively, mange or distemper might eliminate the coyotes, which could result in increased deer numbers (unless these are kept in check by hunting – Steve Yancho, Resource Management Specialist at Sleeping Bear Dunes, pers. commun.). Hunting is *not* currently allowed at **Indiana Dunes** National Lakeshore, **Mississippi National River** and Recreational Area, **Isle Royale** National Park, **Grand Portage** National Monument, and **Voyageurs** National Park. Though, resource managers at Grand Portage believe that deer numbers within the 710-acre park are being kept in check by intense hunting in the surrounding tribal lands (D. Cooper – Chief of Resource Management at Grand Portage, pers. commun.).

Pictured Rocks lies along the Lake Superior snow-belt which has kept deer densities low there (3 per km^2 during snow free months and 0 deer during winters; J. Belant – Supervisory Biologist at Pictured Rocks, pers. commun.). Nevertheless, resource managers there express concerns about how deer numbers might increase with warming temperatures. The most northern GLKN park, Voyageurs, lies close to the northern range limit for white-tailed deer and has deer densities that ranged from 5.1 – 8.6 per km^2 in 2005 (Minnesota DNR 2005, 2006). Comparably, the most southern Network park, Indiana Dunes, has sustained far higher densities of deer (up to 20 deer per km^2 at least locally).

Deer do not occur on **Isle Royale**, but moose (*Alces alces andersoni*) so populations are high and are having a clear impact on patterns of tree regeneration (Snyder and Janke 1976, Brandner et al. 1990). In general, moose prefer balsam fir (*Abies balsamea*), suppressing fir growth and thus recruitment to the canopy (Brandner et al. 1990). However, deer can also affect fir regeneration (Michael 1992) and ungulate effects on fir in general probably increase with decreasing fir density. There is a remarkable and long history of monitoring the impacts of moose foraging on Isle Royale. Peter Jordan of the University of Minnesota established permanent monitoring plots from the early 1960s to the mid-1990s that were designed to explore the impact of moose on vegetation (Jordan et al. 1993). The GLKN is currently collaborating with Jordan to compile this wealth of data into a useable database for further synthesis and additional publications. We concur that researchers should continue to monitor a subset of these plots in an effort separate from and additional to the plots being monitored by the GLKN for changes in vegetation and associated Vital Signs, including ungulate browse.

Moose populations are now declining drastically on Isle Royale, from 2,500 in 1995 to about 650 in 2008 (Jones 2008). Here, moose are isolated from threats that exist elsewhere in Minnesota including cars, hunters, and the parasites carried by deer. Nevertheless, populations across NE Minnesota are declining about 10% per year with pregnancy rates only a bit more than half normal for moose and mortality rates 2-3x average rates in the past (Mark Lenarz, Minnesota DNR, quoted in Jones 2008).

Because we lack a full understanding of many ecosystem changes that have and are taking place (Magnuson 1990), we need to place efforts to monitor deer impacts in a broader context. Sustained research efforts like that of P. Jordan on the plant communities and moose populations on Isle Royale since the 1960s provide a valuable source of information. Likewise, on the Apostle Islands, we benefit greatly by having access to the historical data of Beals et al. (1960) providing baseline data from 1958 on plant community composition and deer impacts. Such studies allow us to incorporate a broader understanding of plant community dynamics including historical disturbances into our efforts to assess, and address, deer impacts. We conclude that sustained efforts to monitor deer impacts should be coupled to routine vegetation monitoring efforts so each effort benefits from the context and understanding provided by the other. Such linkages would also help us to track and understand the spatial and temporal scales of deer impacts.

Threats Posed by Ungulate Herbivory

History of Concerns with Ungulate Browsing and Overabundance

White-tailed deer are native herbivores that have co-evolved with native plant communities throughout their range. After the last glaciers retreated northward in North America, plant communities, herbivores, and predators established a dynamic equilibrium. Since then, deer, predator populations, and plant communities have fluctuated. Deer populations, however, likely remained at or below an ecological carrying capacity due to sparse food and hunting by predators including Native Americans. Ecological carrying capacity is a level of deer abundance where plant communities are sustainable (Redford 1992). European settlement had substantial impacts on deer populations. First, hunting with guns drastically reduced deer populations to the point of extirpation in many areas. Second, widespread landscape transformations and predator removal set in motion conditions that would eventually allow deer populations to increase far above historical levels. The conversion of forests, savannahs and prairies to agriculture, timber production, and urban and suburban development all increase the forage available to deer (Côté et al. 2004). Game protection laws in early 20th century further contributed to white-tailed deer population growth to the point of obvious overabundance in many areas.

Evidence of deer overabundance came by the 1930's when Aldo Leopold began to speak out about the dangers of high deer densities denuding landscapes of tree seedlings and cover (Leopold 1933, 1943a, b, 1946). He was particularly concerned by his observations of overgrazing on the Kaibab plateau north of the Grand Canyon and in the managed Austrian and German forests he visited in 1935 (Leopold 1936). He warned clearly and repeatedly that unchecked ungulate populations could have severe and long-lasting impacts on plant communities and labored long, hard, and mostly unsuccessfully to shift deer management in Wisconsin. He also pointed out that deer themselves would eventually suffer if overbrowsing was sustained as favored deer food plants dwindled in abundance, increasing starvation particularly in the winter.

Overabundant deer populations are populations above an ecological carrying capacity that cause extensive impacts on the vegetation and eventually ecosystem function (McShea et al. 1997). In forested landscapes, overabundant deer strongly affect forest species composition, tree regeneration, vertical structure, understory species dynamics, species diversity, the prevalence of invasive plant species, and probably nutrient cycling.

Deer alter species diversity and composition because plant species differ in their palatability and their resistance or tolerance to browsing. Some plant species are highly defended or have morphological or life history traits that allow them to avoid or physically resist browsing. Plant defenses include physical defenses (e.g., thorns and toughness) and chemical defenses (e.g., toxins, silica, and digestion inhibitors). Some plant species have low nutritional value (Hartley and Jones 1997). Plants also reduce the effects of browsing through life history traits such as the ability to re-sprout after repeated browsing or grow quickly to a height where their leaves and meristems are out of the reach of deer. Grasses and sedges grow continuously from low basal meristems allowing them to tolerate high levels of grazing. When deer are sufficiently abundant, though, fast-growing, palatable species often cannot avoid herbivory when they are small and still within the "molar zone" (i.e., 20-140 cm tall) when plants are vulnerable to deer browsing (Kitterage et al. 1995).

Susceptible species often lack physical and chemical defenses to deter browsing or have life history traits that make them vulnerable. Some species either cannot re-sprout after being browsed once or cannot recover quickly enough from the amount of carbon lost from repeated browsing. In forest understories, shaded environments slow growth, stranding shade-tolerant species for many years in the vulnerable molar zone. Species that cannot tolerate or resist deer usually succumb. In addition, many long-lived understory herbs take a decade or more to grow before reproducing. Herbivory at any point during this long juvenile phase may doom plants to death before they can set seed. Even if they do survive, their maturing flowers and fruits are often conspicuous and vulnerable to being preferentially grazed. If such impacts are widespread and sustained, seed sources are eliminated and populations will decline. In contrast, well-defended and otherwise resistant or tolerant species will persist or increase under these conditions, further reducing opportunities for deer-sensitive species to re-colonize these sites. In such situations, the continued presence of some plants may belie the reproductive failures and ecological extinction of these species (Redford 1992). That is, once species decline to low population numbers, they become more vulnerable to both stochastic forces and possible Allee effects (negative population growth) associated with restricted pollination, dispersal, or seedling establishment.

Impacts on Woody Trees and Shrubs

Although white-tailed deer consume a wide variety of foods including flowers, herbaceous plants, acorns, carrion, and fish, the staple of their diet particularly in winter consists of woody browse (Johnson et al. 1995). Deer are considered generalists but also have clear preferences among food plants. As a result, abundant deer have substantial impacts on the composition of forest vegetation. For example, because deer like to consume oak mast (acorns) and oak seedlings, they tend to reduce oak populations over time. Among woody plants, deer in the region are known to prefer conifers, particularly in winter, including northern white cedar (*Thuja occidentalis*), eastern hemlock (*Tsuga candensis*), and Canada yew (*Taxus canadensis*). Although cedar and hemlock can eventually grow tall enough to escape browsing, this takes many years under shady conditions. Yew never outgrows its vulnerability to deer making it particularly susceptible to heavy browsing even for just a few years. This sensitivity makes it one of the clearest indicators for discriminating between deer-dominated landscapes and habitats where deer are scarce or absent (as seen clearly among the Apostle islands – Judziewicz and Koch 1993).

Preferential browsing by deer thus tends to shift forest composition towards species that tolerate or resist browsing (Horsley et al. 2003) Ecologists have been documenting the effects of deer on forest regeneration for decades (Ross et al. 1970). Perhaps most conspicuously, deer shift the composition of hemlock dominated forests from eastern hemlock (*Tsuga canadensis*) to sugar maple (*Acer saccharum*) and other hardwoods (as seen around the Sylvania Wilderness in the Ottawa National Forest – Davis et al. 1996). Although deer eat both species, deer prefer hemlock over sugar maple especially in winter. Hemlock's slower growth restricts its ability to rapidly exploit light gaps in contrast to maple which can resprout vigorously (Anderson and Loucks 1979). Deer also tend to browse off male Canada yew (*Taxus canadensis*) cones before they release pollen, limiting pollination and seed set in the females (Allison 1990b).

Such shifts in species composition affect forest dynamics and alter successional pathways. Abundant deer can stall succession, accelerate succession, or alter its pathways (Davidson 1993; Côté et al. 2004). In early successional grassy old-fields, deer remove pioneer tree species delaying the time until a closed forest canopy develops (Inouye et al. 1994). In mid or late successional forests, moderate or severe disturbances typically permit pioneer species to regenerate and become established but abundant deer can remove many of these pioneers allowing late-successional deer tolerant species to persist (Davidson 1993). In this case, late successional species can come to dominate sites sooner than if deer were scarce or there were no disturbance. Abundant deer populations thus strongly affect plant communities and successional trajectories.

The largest impact deer have on trees is preventing some species from regenerating. Abundant deer in New England have the strongest impact on hemlock and black birch, but the regeneration of all species was curtailed when deer densities reach about 60 km^{-2} (Kitterage et al. 1995). In Pennsylvania, Massachusetts and Wisconsin, deer densities of 7-12 deer km^{-2} prevent the regeneration of at least some tree species (deCalesta and Stout 1997). In Wisconsin, winter deer browsing depresses the regeneration of eastern hemlock (*Tsuga canadensis*) and northern white-cedar (*Thuja occidentalis*) because both evergreens are important winter foods for deer (Rooney et al. 2000; Rooney et al. 2002; Waller et al. 1996). Deer browse on hardwoods mostly in the spring. Deer browsing strongly limit the regeneration of northern red oak (*Quercus rubra*) and yellow birch (*Betula alleghaniensis*) seedlings (Rooney and Waller 2003). Although overabundant deer clearly reduce or eliminate tree regeneration on local scales, other factors also affect patterns of tree regeneration (Didier and Porter 2003).

Forests have three main vertical layers: *the overstory* or canopy; *the midstory* including shrubs and sapling-sized trees; and *the understory* which includes all plants less than about 1 m tall. The 'herbaceous layer' strictly refers to the herbaceous (non-woody) plants present but is often used loosely to refer to all short-statured individuals including regenerating shrubs and trees. Deer reduce seedling and sapling height and density (Opperman and Merenlender 2000). In forests where deer have been abundant for many years, deer removed the shrubs and saplings in the midstory and understory leaving an open, *park-like* structure. People often interpret these areas as being peaceful, neat, and pretty because they can easily walk and see through the trees for a long distance. Sometimes the forest floor will be blanketed with a single, low-growing species such as fern, adding to people's aesthetic perception (e.g., George and Bazzaz 1999). These "fern parks" where deer have removed much of the understory, shrub and sapling layer, however, may not be self-sustaining because trees are not regenerating (Horsley et al.

2003. As overstory trees die and fall, there are no young trees to replace them. The canopy eventually breaks up as the density of overstory trees declines.

Impacts on Herbaceous Species

Although deer are considered browsers, they consume herbaceous species as well. In spring and early summer, deer quickly switch from their woody diets to include a majority of more nutritious herbaceous plants (McCaffery et al. 1974; Skinner and Telfer 1974; Stormer & Bauer 1980). Herbaceous plants remain in the molar zone making them especially susceptible to deer herbivory. Forest herbaceous layers also support the most plant diversity, giving considerable latitude for diet preferences to be expressed. The herbaceous layer is also highly dynamic spatially and temporally relative to the other forest layers (Gilliam and Roberts 2003). Herbivory in the understory also affects overall forest dynamics as even tree seedlings must pass through the herb layer's ecological filter. That is, herbivory influences the composition and competitive dynamics among plants and thus patterns of forest succession.

The herb layer includes many highly palatable and preferred species. Deer particularly like to consume nutritious flowers and fruit. Thus, even when deer do not remove entire plants, they can depress reproduction. As a result, sensitive herb species become rare or extirpated from forests (Rooney and Waller 2003; Rooney et al. 2004). Sensitive species share traits that include long life span, low yearly reproduction, and a lack of effective anti-herbivore compounds. This group includes species that humans appreciate such as orchids, lobeliads, and lilies like *Trillium* (Miller et al. 1992). Many studies verify that abundant deer contribute to the declines we observe in many herbaceous species and overall herb diversity (Anderson 1994; Augustine et al. 1998; McGraw and Furedi 2005; Patel and Rapport 2000; Rooney and Waller 2003; Stokstad, 2005; Stockton et al. 2005).

As already noted, deer sometimes create park-like conditions within forests by removing native shrubs, tree seedlings and saplings, and most herbaceous species. Under heavy deer herbivory, forests can come to have understories dominated by one or a few very abundant species tolerant of or resistant to deer herbivory. Such species include: exotic invasives (e.g., garlic mustard; *Alliaria petiolata* or Asian silt grass; *Microstegium vimineum*); native herbaceous species (e.g., Jack-in-the-pulpit; *Arisaema triphyllum*, enchanters nightshade; *Circaea lutetiana)*; woody natives like Virginia creeper (*Parthenocissus quinquefolia*); certain native shrubs (e.g., choke cherry; *Prunus virginiana*); and exotic shrub species like common and European buckthorn (*Rhamnus cathartica* and *Rhamnus frangula*). Interestingly, all of these dominant species have increased dramatically in abundance in the lake states over the last 50 years (Rooney et al. 2004; Wiegmann and Waller 2006a). Concurrent with these increases for a few species has been a conspicuous decline in overall native plant diversity.

Remarkably, deer also appear to be having negative impacts even on unpalatable plant species in some forests. Heckel and Kalisz (2008) found that Jack-in-the-pulpit (*Arisaema triphyllum*) had reduced growth, plant size, flowering, and seed rain in proportion to deer impacts on favored browse species. They attributed these impacts to drier, more compacted soils revealing that deer impacts may extend farther than previously thought.

Deer Impacts on Other Animals
By removing the midstory and understory, deer indirectly affect many other animals (Rooney and Waller 2003). For example, overabundant deer caused both ground-dwelling and shrub-nesting bird populations to decline as the birds became more exposed to predators and lost nest sites (deCalesta 1994; McShea and Rappole 2000; Allombert et al. 2005a). The loss of the midstory and understory can also increase predation on small mammals (Flowerdew and Ellwood 2001) and alter invertebrate populations (Suominen 1999; Suominen et al. 1999; Allombert et al. 2005b). There are probably many other impacts on animals that have yet to be detected or analyzed.

Potential Impacts on the Spread of Exotic Species
Introduced species have evolved in one area but humans have moved them to another area either intentionally or incidentally. About 10% of introduced species establish sustainable populations and we term these species "exotic." Most exotic species are ruderal or weedy and maintain populations in highly disturbed areas such as roadsides, in campgrounds, and old-fields among other locations. These species become part of the community but their presence does not alter the overall nature of the native community. Roughly 10% of exotic species subsequently become extremely abundant and we term these species invasive. Invasive species often replace native species sometimes through competition because invasives are better able to exploit and use resources. Other invasives become very abundant by producing toxic chemicals that reduce the abundances of other plant species or deters herbivory and disease (Callaway and Ridenour 2004). Invasive species have strong impacts on ecosystem processes and function (Shea and Chesson 2002). For example, invasive plants can alter fire return times and fire intensity, alter microbial communities both plant symbiants and detritus microbes, and reduce tree regeneration.

In addition to these direct effects on native communities, white-tail deer also have indirect effects on native plant communities via interactions with other factors. First, deer and invasive species interactions can produce a double-whammy effect on native plant communities. Deer can cause apparent competition when they selectively favor foraging on native species over invasives. In such cases, natives are removed or reduced in abundance, expanding the resources available for less browsed invasives to use. Second, white-tailed deer can increase the spread of invasive species through the dispersal of their seeds. Deer disperse seeds of invasive species either by carrying seeds on their fur or by ingesting mature seeds and ripe fruit and depositing viable seeds in fecal scat piles (Myers et al. 2004). Third, the impacts of deer browsing depend on plant density as well as deer density. For example, when the native wood nettle, *Laportea canadensis,* was abundant in woodlots in S Minnesota, deer browsing had little affect on its populations. In contrast, in forests where this species was less abundant, deer browsing sharply reduced its density switching the herbaceous community to an alternative stable state (Augustine et al. 1998).

Most invasive species that thrive within the range of white-tailed deer have a trait in common: the ability to tolerate or resist white-tailed deer herbivory. Case in point, Garlic mustard and Buckthorn, two of the most invasive species in the lake states, are species deer avoid consuming. A recent study in New Jersey and Pennsylvania (Eschtruth and Battles 2008) found support for the enemy release hypothesis in that three exotic plants (*Microstegium vimineum, Alliaria petiolata,* and *Berberis thunbergii*) gained a competitive advantage in the presence of more deer. They found that deer herbivory accelerates the invasion of these exotic plants, an effect they attributed to resisting herbivory (though trampling or soil nutrient mechanisms were not ruled out).

Do Deer Affect Nutrient Cycling?

Overabundant white-tailed deer may also alter nutrient cycling. To date, this subject is under studied, but there is direct and indirect evidence that abundant deer could have substantial effects, accelerating nutrient cycling by shifting carbon and nutrients from plant biomass into deer biomass and feces that enter the soil. In some areas with elevated deer populations dung beetles are more prevalent than where deer are less abundant (Brian Pederson, Dickinson College, pers. commun.). By converting plant biomass accumulating in the understory and midstory into soil biomass, deer may be shifting forest ecosystems from a primary production-based food web to detritus-based food web.

Ungulate herbivory in the Serengeti is known to accelerate nutrient cycling (McNaughton 1976; McNaughton 1985) by increasing tissue loss, which in turn increases plant uptake of nutrients. Richtie et al. (1998), however, found that herbivores including deer can decelerate nutrient cycling because deer feed on nutrient rich tissue increasing the dominance of plants with nutrient-poor tissue or defense compounds (Ritchie et al. 1998). Such plant species have leaves with a higher lignin concentration, higher C:N ratio, or both (Wiegmann and Waller *submitted*). In this case, nutrients remain tied-up in the leaf litter longer and mineralize more slowly than in species with less lignin and lower C:N ratios (Hobbs 1996). Thus, nutrient cycling is altered and site productivity may decline (Rooney and Waller 2003).

The Consequent Need to Monitor Impacts

The number, diversity, complexity, and significance of ungulate impacts on forest plant communities make it important to monitor their impacts in the upper Great Lakes National Parks. These include all the individual impacts summarized above as well as the broader specter that deer could be driving forests in the region into an alternate stable state that could be very difficult to reverse (Stromayer and Warren 1997).

Monitoring could take any of several forms and should therefore be designed carefully to maximize the value of the data returned given the limited monitoring funds available. Ideally, an ungulate monitoring program would be efficient in terms of time and money, simple to administer, sustained, and capable of delivering reliable results soon enough to allow timely shifts in ungulate and/or forest management to minimize the many deleterious impacts outlined above. This is particularly important for the Parks, as hunting options may be limited, significant public relations issues need to be addressed, and the impacts of overbrowsing can be severe, long-lasting, and difficult-to-reverse.

Continued monitoring programs are needed to fully assess the short- and longer-term ecological impacts of ungulate browsing. While some populations and species appear resilient and able to recover quickly from ungulate browsing, other populations and species appear sensitive to browsing and quite slow to recover, particularly in fragmented habitats. As data accumulate in monitoring programs, we will be in a better position to evaluate how ungulate browsing affects particular plant species and the communities they occupy and the conditions that favor their recovery. Such a program, however, relies on having replicated exclosures and/or some other spatial variation in ungulate abundance.

There is also the particular opportunity in the NPS Vital Signs program to 'piggy-back' the monitoring of ungulate impacts onto the routine vegetation surveys and monitoring that have already begun in the region. That is, little further effort may be required once botanically trained survey arrive at a site to obtain the additional data needed to gauge browsing impacts. This would thus be efficient. However, efficiently integrating browsing impacts monitoring with the vegetation surveys and monitoring will also require careful attention to choose the correct variables to monitor (Section 4.) and to decide how best to combine and analyze these data (Section 5.).

Approaches to Assessing Ungulate Threats

In assessing deer browse impacts, several options exist. These include assessing deer densities, the direct impacts of deer on woody and herbaceous species, and their indirect impacts on forest community structure and composition. Each method has its advantages and disadvantages for assessing browse impacts, leading some authors to suggest using several methods simultaneously. Monitoring ungulate impacts on woody plants typically involves either directly tracking stature or the number of browsed twigs or indirect inferences of browsing based on demography (e.g., the relative proportions of individuals in various size or age classes). The former better characterize transient and recent impacts, while the latter provide a more longer-term picture that integrates past ungulate impacts over time.

Because it is conventional to assume that deer impacts are proportional to deer densities, we begin with a brief review of methods used to estimate deer densities. However, because counting deer is usually expensive, cumbersome, and prone to inaccuracies, we focus more on methods to assess the direct and indirect impacts of deer by measuring features of forest plant communities. We review both the use of individual indicator species and collective or community responses. An overview of using fenced exclosures to experimentally assess deer impacts concludes this section.

Estimating deer population densities

Historically, wildlife biologists placed considerable emphasis on obtaining estimates of deer density as a prelude to evaluating deer impacts and deciding on how best to manage deer. Knowing whether deer populations are increasing or decreasing would appear to be of obvious use in judging whether to implement changes in deer management.

Historically, much of the interest in estimating deer densities also reflects hunter interest. It would also be useful to have estimates of deer abundance to compare with direct or indirect estimates of deer impacts. If these correspond, it may be possible to cross-calibrate the methods so as to use vegetation impacts to estimate deer densities. Various groups (e.g., in S France and Pennsylvania), however, are moving toward the idea of replacing direct estimates of deer densities with vegetation-based methods that focus on impacts (Latham et al. 2008). Given the costs of difficulty in obtaining fine-scale estimates of deer density, this would be of great use.

Most state Departments of Natural Resources make efforts to estimate deer numbers, typically on a fairly coarse scale. Efforts to enumerate ungulates have historically been based on counts of:
- the animals seen (e.g., at night from roads using lights)
- trail density
- fecal scat groups

Variations of these direct counts include distance-based methods (e.g., Thomas et al. 2005). Less direct methods based on sex and age ratios and kill statistics (like the Sex-Age-Kill (SAK) model used in Wisconsin – see URL: http://dnr.wi.gov/org/land/wildlife/hunt/deer) now tend to dominate, despite tending to spark controversy. Because direct counts require lots of field effort, they are becoming rare. In addition, the recent audit of Wisconsin's **SAK model** indicated that the estimates generated by this technique typically have an error of +/- 100% within particular DMU's. These counts are also at a coarse spatial scale representing regional densities, the type of information provided by the Wisconsin Department of Natural Resources. These averages do not necessary reflect local densities, however, which vary depending on landowner, land use, and hunting pressure.

Finer scale data on deer densities would provide a better basis for making resource management decisions. Such fine-scale data can come from **aerial surveys**, local pellet scat data, or **automated cameras**. Aerial surveys typically use IR imagery in the winter when leaves are off the trees and cold temperatures provide better contrast for deer thermal radiation (see, for example, http://www.aitscan.com/animalfindir.php). These surveys are also expensive, however, and less complete and accurate in areas with dense evergreen foliage cover. Methods clearly differ in cost and effectiveness. Work by Potvin et al. on aerial surveys found accuracies of 64-83% with double-count methods (Potvin and Breton 2005), or estimates with confidence intervals that encompassed pellet-count results (Potvin et al. 2002). With these studies they conclude that aerial surveys are effective, and may be as cost effective as other methods.

Counts of **deer fecal pellet groups** represent a common method for estimating deer abundance with a long history of use (Bennett et al. 1940; Batcheler 1975; Rowland et al. 1984). Both Michigan and Wisconsin used pellet group counts for decades to infer deer densities and adjust management practices (until these were deemed too labor intensive and expensive). They have particular value in providing an index of local browsing pressure at a finer scale than, say, SAK results. There is also some controversy about their accuracy, however (Fuller 1991; White 1992). For his master's thesis, Langdon (Langdon 2001) examined pellet surveys, spotlight surveys, and automatic cameras as options in West Virginia. His analysis showed that the least expensive method, pellet surveys, was also the least accurate, while the automatic camera option was the most accurate at estimating deer densities, although the most expensive. This work shows promise for automatic-camera or spotlight surveys, which in combination with DNR estimates from hunting data could provide accurate estimates of deer densities.

A major concern in monitoring deer densities or condition directly is that these variables (even if they could be accurately measured) may not, in themselves, represent accurate or reliable indicators of deer impacts and forest conditions for deer. This reflects the fact that ungulate impacts are often context specific, depending on the availability of browse (which can reflect the history of past browsing), alternative sources of food in the vicinity, and the abundances of various plant species. Thus, our ability to use ungulate densities to infer ungulate impacts in an area is limited and specific to that location and vegetative community. Nevertheless, it could be useful to have data, particularly on trends in ungulate abundance, in order to determine how vegetation and other biotic and abiotic aspects are responding to increases or decreases in browsing. Trend data, whatever the source, can also indicate whether ungulate populations are increasing or decreasing and whether these changes are gradual or rapid. Such information is of clear value and use for land management.

If we are more interested in deer impacts than the deer themselves, we should ask whether it makes sense to try to estimate deer densities themselves at all. As already pointed out, estimating deer densities usually entails considerable time and expense and is prone to inaccuracies. In addition, any efforts to estimate deer density in order to adjust deer management to reduce deer impacts rests on the implicit assumption that deer impacts scale with deer density. If, however, deer impacts respond as much to vegetation type and the densities of various plants as they do to deer density itself (or if deer impacts are highly heterogeneous in time and space), it makes more sense to simply monitor the deer impacts themselves and adjust deer management activities accordingly. Interestingly, this is exactly the conclusion reached recently by a group of experts hired by the Pennsylvania Bureau of Forestry and Game Commission (Latham et al. 2008).

Direct impacts on woody plants and forbs

One of the most apparent indicators of ungulate browse are the conspicuous "browse lines" that appear on many conifers following browsing. Although easy to identify and perhaps even quantify, they do not provide ideal indicators in that by the time browse lines appear, impacts have probably been underway for years. Browse lines also persist for many years, providing a 'lagging' indicator. Methods that provide more contemporary records of browsing often involve using seedlings, saplings or shrubs as living "phytometers." Such phytometers can provide earlier warnings of deer impacts than browse lines.

Woody plants leave physical records of past growth and browsing which can often be read in terms of twig damage, extension, and branching (Table 1). For example, the **Sugar Maple Browse Index (SMBI)** provides a simple method to estimate local deer browsing pressure from the proportion of browsed twigs on sugar maple (*Acer saccharum*) (Frelich and Lorimer 1985). The SMBI relies on shade-tolerant sugar maple seedlings and saplings because these tend to be abundant and widely dispersed, providing a more convenient phytometer for deer browsing intensity than more favored or more sparsely distributed species. The index is based on the overall proportion of browsed terminal sugar maple twigs located 30–200 cm above the ground as judged from the ratio of browsed to total twigs on 12–20 maple saplings per site. Rooney and Waller (2001) used red oak seedlings (*Quercus rubra*) as phytometers. They found that seedling densities drop precipitously as browsing pressure increases from low to intermediate, indicating that red oak regeneration is strongly limited by deer and can be used as a phytometer. Other woody plants studied in connection to deer browse include *Taxus canadensis*, whose original high frequency in the region reflected low historic deer population (Balgooyen and Waller 1995). Of these methods, the SMBI is the most widely used. It has been shown to correlate with changes in deer browse impacts on other species like the number of larger hemlock seedlings (Rooney and Waller 1998).

Other methods also use tree saplings and shrubs to indicate direct physical browse impacts. Vila et al. (2001, 2003), for example, used dendrochronology to tie bud scale scars, scars from antler scrapes, and historical variation in growth rates to historic fluctuations in deer densities on the Queen Charlotte islands, Canada. These methods provide a valuable technique for inferring past ungulate densities and impacts. However, they may be less useful for inferring contemporary impacts. They are also too time consuming and elaborate to be cheap or performed quickly in the field. Although direct tallies of browse damage on herbaceous species' leaves and stems can be used, herbivory often completely removes plants leaving no trace of herbivory. We discuss ways to indirectly assess ungulate impacts using herbaceous species below.

Two indices of deer browsing have been developed in Europe to assess the impacts of roe deer (*Capreolus capreolus*) as an alternative to estimating deer density directly. Both of these are unusual in that they are based on browsing on all available browse species present rather then any particular species. Guibert (1997) developed the **Index of browsing Pressure on the Flora** (IPF) for tracking changes in browsing pressure through time at a site (not comparisons among sites). He defined the IPF as the ratio of the number of browsed woody plant species to the total number of woody plant species present at a site:

$$IPF = \frac{\sum_i \sum_j C_{ij}}{\sum_i \sum_j P_{ij}}$$

Where C_{ij} refers to the browsing of woody plant species **j** on plot **i** and P_{ij} is the presence of this woody species **j** on plot **i**. The sums are over all species and plots, and he used plots 3.57m in diameter (40 m^2). Guibert restricted his surveys to woody species present in >10% of the plots. He considered a species browsed if >5% of its shoots in the molar zone (<1.2 m) were eaten with surveys typically occurring just before the resumption of vegetative growth in the Spring (allowing browsing impacts to accumulate, much like scat groups, over the winter). Morellet et al. (2003) tested this index for its replicability across 14 sets of observers on 50 plots. Estimated IPF ranged from 15% to 46% with a highly significant observer x plot effect. Such large observer effects and bias handicap the use of this index. They also pointed out that the presence and browsing of various species are not independent of each other, also possibly leading to bias.

Table 1. Range of deer impacts on plants and associated potential indicators.

Group or indicator	Number or density	Size or height	Reproductive condition	Direct Damage
Trees	Oak and hemlock seedlings (Rooney & Waller 2001)	Hemlock (Rooney and Dress 1997)		Sugar Maple Browse Index (Frelich & Lorimer 1985) Morellet Index - Morellet et al. 2001
Shrubs	Yew (*Taxus*)	Yew patch size or cover	Damage to male yew cones (Allison 1990)	Yew
Herbaceous Forbs	Maianthemum canadensis (Rooney 1997)	*Trillium grandiflorum* (Augustine and Frelich 1998, Anderson 1994)	*Clintonia borealis* (Balgooyen & Waller 1995)	*Chelone glabra* (Williams et al. 2000)
	Laportea canadensis (Augustine et. al 1998)	*Clintonia borealis* (Balgooyen & Waller 1995)	*Maianthemum canadensis* (Rooney 1997)	
		Maianthemum canadensis (Rooney 1997)	*Trillium grandiflorum* (Augustine and Frelich 1998)	
		Osmorhiza claytonii (Webster et al. 2001)	*Arisaema triphyllum* (Fletcher et al. 2001)	
		Arisaema triphyllum (Webster et al. 2001)	*Uvularia* sp. (Fletcher et al. 2001)	
		Actaea pachypoda (Webster et al. 2001)	*Smilacina* sp. (Fletcher et al. 2001)	
			I sp. (Fletcher et al. 2001)	
			I(Fletcher et al. 2001)	

As an alternative, Morellet et al. (2001, 2003) introduced a new simple index for tallying browse damage on woody plants. They developed their index from a statistical (Boolean) model and calibrated it carefully against densities of roe deer in France (estimated via direct observations) during a period when populations increased greatly ($r^2 = 0.85$. They define the **Browsing Index** (*BI*) using a Bayesean approach where the posterior distribution has an expected value of:

$$\mathbf{BI} = (1 + n_c) / (2 + n_p)$$

Where $\mathbf{n}_c$ is the number of plots with any evidence of browsing present and $\mathbf{n}_p$ is the total number of plots with any woody species present <1.2m tall. Note that this index is again based on all available browse species present rather than particular species. (They found *Rubus* sp. to be particularly widespread and useful.) They found that although species-specific browsing rates differed widely, their browsing index closely tracked the roe deer population size. They concluded that their index provides an efficient and reliable tool for monitoring deer impacts that was sensitive to changes in population density. They recommend a sample size of 150 plots of $1m^2$ spaced evenly across study areas that ranged from a few to >100 ha. As its statistical properties are also well characterized, it is straightforward to make comparisons over space and time. *We therefore consider this index to be worth serious consideration for use in the Vital Signs program.*

Indirect Impacts on Size, Demography, and Indicator Species

When direct measures of browse impacts are not available, or when multiple measurements are needed to make results stronger, one can also resort to indirect estimates of ungulate impacts. These can be based on demography (e.g., the distribution of size or age classes), flowering / fruiting condition, or shifts in forest structure. As ungulate densities increase, certain size classes (often a proxy for age-classes) are usually hit harder than others. Seedlings and shrubs within deer feeding range often suffer highly reduced numbers or can be completely absent. The number of seedlings and small saplings can be counted and compared with the abundance of larger size classes among stands known or thought to differ in deer browse intensity (Anderson and Loucks 1979). In this way, the number of seedlings and saplings in progressively larger size classes can be used to examine how various biotic and abiotic environmental factors including deer combine to affect seedling establishment and survival to subsequent size classes (Waller et al. 1996; Rooney et al. 2000, 2002).

Eventually, chronic deer browsing will also affect overall forest structure. Sustained deer browsing can result in 'fern parks' - open, shrub-free forests with fern-dominated understory that are biologically impoverished (Rooney 2001). Using a historical survey, Rooney and Dress (Rooney and Dress 1997) showed that beech stands in Pennsylvania lost most (59% and 80%) species of their ground flora between 1929 and 1995. They attributed many of these losses to direct and indirect effects of deer. Quantifying the shift from dense, diverse understories to open woodlands is difficult without historical data, as there is no baseline for comparison, and defining how 'open' a stand is can be subjective depending on the observer.

It is often of particular value to monitor particular indicator species known to be palatable to ungulates or rarer species (or age/size classes) of conservation concern. However, their rarity also makes it inherently more difficult to obtain sample sizes large enough to provide adequate statistical power to reliably infer impacts. Although other herbaceous plants may leave no physical record of past herbivory, they can provide abundant, widespread phytometers for inferring ungulate impacts. We can, in particular, use the presence, abundance, size (typically height), and flowering condition of particular plants to infer the current and recent impacts of ungulates (Anderson 1994, Rooney 1997, Rooney and Waller 2001). While looking at overall shifts in composition can give a picture of indirect deer impacts, another option is to target certain species known to be sensitive to deer browse (see Table 1). Tracking their fluctuations in frequency and the overall height of the population provides another option for indirectly measuring ungulate impact, and a number of species have been considered. This differs from studying direct impacts in that browse does not have to be observed directly – the characteristics or density of the plants on the site are compared to areas with a higher or lower deer density.

In the Allegheny region of Pennsylvania, Canada mayflower (*Maianthemum canadensis*) grows to larger sizes, at three times the density, and flowers more frequently on top of tall boulders compared with nearby short boulders (Rooney 1997). This difference seems clearly attributable to deer herbivory. Another study on herb height (Anderson 1994) found that large-leaf trillium (*Trillium grandiflorum*) increases in stem height with decreased deer browse. Anderson compared the stem height to the percent cover of herbs that were browsed, and found a negative correlation which indicates that trillium can serve as an indicator of deer browse. Webster et al. (2005) found similar connections between trillium height and deer browse impacts in Great Smoky Mountain National Park. Webster et al. (2001) also looked at height for three other species, sweet cicely (*Osmorhiza claytonii*), jack-in-the-pulpit (*Arisaema triphyllum*), and white baneberry (*Actaea pachypoda*), and compared it to deer browse. They found that the species provided reasonable indicators of deer impacts. Additionally, Balgooyen and Waller (1995) studied blue-bead lily (*Clintonia borealis*), an important spring food for deer. They found that the frequency, scape height, leaf number and pedicels per umbel decreased with higher deer density. These findings make blue-bead lily a candidate indicator of deer browsing pressure. Fletcher et al. (2001a) examined a number of individual species and genera, including *Uvularia* sp., *Smilacina* sp., *Polygonatum* sp., *Orchis spectabilis*, and *Arisaema triphyllum* by noting population and reproductive activity. In all cases, the reproductive activity was negatively correlated with increasing deer density. Given this, they suggest that reproductive activity could also be a way to measure the severity of deer impacts, especially among the studied species (Fletcher et al. 2001b). Augustine and Frelich (1998) used *Laportea canadensis* to measure how ungulate effects vary in response to both deer and plant density, potentially creating alternative stable states that depend on the history of herbivory. Additional species suggested by Williams et al. (2000) include *Chelone glabra* (turtle-head), *Aster divaricatus*, *A. prenanthoides* and *Impatiens capensis*, all of which were preferentially browsed by deer in the eastern U.S. Their findings point to the use of more than one species as an indicator to give a more accurate picture of deer impacts in an area.

Some studies have found that herbaceous species' characteristics such as height and reproductive activity are not well correlated with other measures of deer impacts. Kirschbaum and Anacker (2005) working in Pennsylvania looked at *Maianthemum canadensis* and *Trillium grandiflorum* heights and reproduction and compared them to browse on woody species. Although height and flowering were affected, they did not correlate with the level of woody species browse. The authors concluded that while deer can impact herbaceous species, direct browsing on woody stems provides a better predictor of deer densities and impacts. This result may also reflect the spotty nature of deer herbivory and associated high variance.

Studies like this point to an important issue: in order to be effective, methods should be tested against one another to determine which is the most accurate. In different areas, other techniques may be favored over others given the presence of woody (e.g., *A. saccharum*) or herbaceous indicator species, hypothesized deer densities, and site history. Another point about indicator species is that indicator species should be selected based on their sensitivity to changes in deer density but the changes do not have to be negative (Rooney 2001). As indicated above, graminoids and ferns increase in abundance and could be used especially in areas were browse-sensitive plants have been wiped out.

Given these past studies, species in the genera *Trillium*, *Polygonatum*, *Clintonia*, and *Uvularia* are all potential candidates for observing direct impact of deer. All are easy to identify long-lived perennials. They also share a determinate pattern of flowering and must reach a minimum threshold size to flower, providing the opportunity to use several traits: abundance, size (height), clipped leaves or stems, and flowering or fruiting condition as potential indicators of deer herbivory. These were the species studied in our preliminary field project.

Shifts in Forest Composition and Structure

Along similar lines, looking at the shift in plant composition gets rid of the subjective aspect, though this is still dependent on baseline data. In areas where ungulate pressure has been high for a relatively long time, tree composition changes because browse can eliminate trees sensitive to browsing (Blewett 1976). Changes in the understory herb layer shift composition faster than overstory tree composition, though, and it is more effective to look there for indications of deer impacts. Two general trends are found in areas of heavy deer impact: a decline in browse-sensitive forbs and gains of browse-tolerant forbs, such as graminoids (grass and sedge family plants) and ferns

Concerning the first trend, slow-growing plants will be less tolerant of browsing, particularly if such browsing is repeated. Shady forest understory plants including shade-tolerant shrubs and tree seedlings may thus be particularly vulnerable to deer browse. Small spring ephemeral and early summer forest herbs that lose all of their leaves or flowers in a single bite and cannot regrow also tolerate herbivory poorly (Augustine and McNaughton 1998, Augustine and DeCalesta 2003). Where deer are abundant, browsing-intolerant herbs tend to be smaller, less likely to flower, and less likely to survive relative to plants in exclosures (Anderson 1994, Augustine and Frelich 1998, Ruhren and Handel 2000, Fletcher et al. 2001a, Ruhren and Handel 2003). Over time, the density of such intolerant plants tends to decline and populations may be extirpated (Rooney and Dress 1997).

Concerning the second trend, deer herbivory tends to favor grasses and sedges (Wiegmann and Waller 2006), several of which are exotic species in Wisconsin. This is because plants that only lose a small fraction of leaves or flowers, store resources underground, and hide their meristems (as in grasses), or those that regrow quickly via indeterminate growth, tolerate deer herbivory better (Augustine and McNaughton 1998, Wiegmann and Waller 2006). Such species include many annuals, graminoids, deciduous trees and shrubs, and many herbs and forbs that mature in late summer. Thus, as local deer browsing increases in mixed coniferous–deciduous forest stands, understory herb community diversity declines, while ferns, grasses, sedges, and rushes become increasingly dominant.

Declines in palatable species and increases in less-nutritious species support the hypothesis that deer are strongly affecting forest understory communities. Fiber content of plant tissues, in particular, correlated well with differences among sites and species in herbivory and impacts (Wiegmann and Waller, submitted). This suggests that an index based on average plant fiber and protein content at a site could provide a useful indicator of cumulative deer impacts. If deer force overall declines in plant palatability, we might also consider developing a community metric to assess past deer impacts by computing an average of plant nutrition characteristics across most or all species (weighted by their individual abundances at each site). Such an approach reflects recent interest in using plant functional traits to predict community composition and dynamics (Cingolani et al. 2005; Gondard et al. 2003; Mayfield et al. 2006; Roy and de Blois 2006; Suding et al. 2005; Williams et al. 2005).

Observed changes in the nutritional composition of forest communities over time (Wiegmann & Waller, submitted) suggest that we could use such data to construct an index of 'community palatability' to infer past deer impacts and/or track deer impacts over time. This could be readily computed from data on plant community composition, once nutritional characteristics are known. The Waller Lab is already committed to developing a public database to provide these values for many of the more common forest plant species in the region. Such an approach assumes that these nutritional values are relatively stable and vary more among than within species (an hypothesis that is being tested). This community palatability index would compute a weighted average of these species-specific nutritional values, weighting by the relative abundance of species. Excluding data on invasive exotics and problematic species would improve the ability of this index to reflect deer impacts. Such an index thus has the potential to provide a simple and reliable tool for forest and wildlife managers to monitor past and present deer impacts. Such an index could also be used to track how forest understory vegetation recovers following deer control efforts or the construction of fenced exclosures.

Experimental Exclosures

Perhaps the most obvious and rigorously controlled way to evaluate the impacts of ungulates on plant communities is to create fenced enclosures with known deer densities inside or fenced exclosures to exclude deer altogether. Such rigorous control of conditions represents a "gold standard" for judging other methods to infer deer impacts. Fenced areas can also be used to enclose deer at known densities to experimentally assess deer effects at levels other than zero and ambient densities (McShea and Rappole 1997). McCullough's (1984) work in the George Reserve in southern Michigan used a fenced area to assess the dynamics of deer populations and impacts. Controlled grazing experiments using known deer density in enclosures are ideal in providing realistic comparisons for inferring whole community responses to manipulated deer densities (Tilghman 1989, deCalesta 1994, Hester et al. 2000, McShea and Rappole 2000, Cote et al. 2003, Horsley et al. 2003).

Fenced exclosures are of particular value for monitoring ungulate impacts for several reasons. First, they provide direct evidence of ungulate impacts in a controlled experimental setting. Second, such exclosures can be placed to evaluate ungulate impacts on particular species or in particular areas and to assess how these accumulate over time. Third, they can provide visually arresting demonstrations of ungulate impacts with great educational value. To be most useful, exclosures should be replicated and maintained to allow detailed comparisons of community responses over time.

Fenced exclosures provide control by eliminating deer browsing altogether within a confined area and are clearly an effective way to compare areas without deer with surrounding "control" areas subject to ambient deer densities. Such exclosure studies demonstrate, often in a graphic way, just how strongly deer browsing can affect plant growth and tree regeneration and can provide considerable demonstration value for convincing a sometimes skeptical public of the severity of deer impacts. Such studies have existed for more than 50 years and continue to be actively employed to assess deer impacts (Stewart and Burrows 1989, Allison 1990a,b, Anderson and Katz 1993, Ruhren and Dudash 1996, Augustine and Frelich 1998). In our region, for example, exclosures are being used to track the differential survival and growth of hemlock seedlings in response to hare and deer (Alverson and Waller 1997 and unpubl. data). To be most useful for assessing deer effects, such exclosures should be built to exclude deer but not hare or other mammals that can also affect plant growth and survival.

The value of data from exclosures accrues over time as differences become more apparent. However, this time investment also brings obvious costs in the form of rugged construction and continuing maintenance to ensure their integrity. Also, despite the insights that enclosure studies bring into our understanding of deer-forest interactions, they involve binary treatments. That is, exclosures show us an alternate trajectory at a site in the absence of deer. Some criticize exclosures, however, for creating an extreme comparison by completely eliminating ungulates from a study plot. Such conditions, however, are largely outside the natural range of variation of ungulate densities. While exclosures clearly and graphically demonstrate how ungulates affect vegetation structure and composition, they also leave an important gap when the relationships between ungulate density and browsing impacts are non-linear. A second source of confusion occurs when researchers assume that exclosures create the conditions that would occur without browsing. In fact, exclosures illustrate recovery of plots from browsing. Because the browsing history of the plot is not eliminated, changes in the plot strongly reflect local species pools and seed banks (which may have already been depleted from chronic browsing). This may explain why Kraft et al. (2004) found no significant difference in species richness and cover after 5 years in and outside exclosures in the western UP and why Webster et al. (2005) found recovery within exclosures in the Great Smoky Mountains NP to be largely restricted to species able to persist under intense herbivory. Exclosure studies should therefore be combined with other information regarding how gradients in ungulate density affect various elements of diversity.

Analyzing Data Bearing on Ungulate Browse

Monitoring ungulate impacts remains a developing art. Most monitoring in the past has been local and haphazard, focusing on only a few populations or species for a few years and often with a limited agenda. In addition, few methods have been carefully analyzed for their power or cross-calibrated to other methods to test their relative efficacy and accuracy.

Kinds and Quality of Data

As we have seen, data on deer impacts on vegetation range from the anecdotal and through other qualitative assessments to an increasingly quantitative (but still not always reliable) set of indicators. Qualitative descriptions based on direct observations by experienced naturalists should not be discounted or dismissed, particularly when part of historical records, as they often contain valuable information about overall conditions and which species are being affected. Such observations are, however, difficult to compare over sites and time periods (unless the same observer is involved). Simple species lists of what was present in the understory then relative to now can also be highly informative about the probable historic impacts of ungulates (e.g., Rooney and Dress 1997). Such results imply that both routine species lists and especially more complete descriptions of vegetation like those provided by systematic sampling (e.g., Rooney et al. 2004) are valuable for inferring the course of deer impacts and should be valued and preserved for that purpose.

Several more direct and quantitative measures of deer browsing exist but most of these have yet to be rigorously tested or cross-calibrated against other metrics of deer density or browsing impacts (with the exception of Morellet et al.'s 2001 index). This is unfortunate, as knowing how these methods vary among observers, sampling scales, and vegetation types is clearly necessary before we incorporate them into a more systematic long-term monitoring systems. Our own experiences with the SMBI (Frelich and Lorimer 1985) have not been particularly encouraging in this regard. We find these values to have a very large sampling variance and perhaps as a consequence to have little power for predicting declines in most browse-sensitive species or overall plant diversity. However, it may be that there is little relation between variation in sugar maple seedling establishment and deer densities (Didier and Porter 2003).

Methods of Analysis

We do, however, find that responses of many herbaceous and woody species known to be sensitive to deer herbivory tend to covary in consistent ways. For example, we observe systematic decreases in sets of species over the past 50 years that share similar taxonomy or functional traits (Rooney et al. 2004; Wiegmann and Waller 2006). Such results suggest that it may be possible to construct a composite index based on community composition that could serve as an indicator of deer herbivory. The best way to do this would be to obtain enough longer-term data from enclosures and exclosures to chart the dynamics of how various species and groups of species tend to decline over time in response to known densities of deer or intensities of browsing. This would take considerable time and effort, however. An alternative might be to construct a synthetic axis from a Principal Components Analysis of community changes over time in a less rigorously controlled setting such as northern Wisconsin over recent decades or one or more of the Apostle islands that has recently gained deer (Mudrak et al. 2009). Our lab is currently engaged in further analyses of the relationships between plant functional traits and long-term population dynamics for many forest herbs in the region which may also reveal important relationships that could be used to construct a composite index (e.g. based on nutritional value or leaf toughness).

We might also be able to combine data on community species or functional trait composition and relative abundance with more direct data on the incidence of browsed stems and flowers or fruit among the set of indicator species discussed in Section 4.3. At least as a start, we could examine cross-correlations among the browse variables and whether these are high enough to extract a major axis that then might be combined with the major axis based on compositional changes discussed above.

A feature of the Morellet et al. (2001) Browsing Index (BI) was that it was based on binary data, namely the presence and absence of woody plants within a quadrat and the presence of browsing on any such plants. These simple variables allowed a complete Bayesian statistical model to be constructed, characterized, and evaluated for power and potential bias. Such binary variables would be quick to score in the field, another advantage that would allow a greater area to be covered. In addition, although BI takes advantage of all species present, estimates of BI can also be calculated for individual species (if frequent enough) and compared to assess their relative value as indicators (Morellet et al. 2003). This is what led them to conclude that the data from *Rubus* spp. were most representative and responsive. One disadvantage of relying on binary data with this method is that large sample sizes are needed (they recommend 150 one m^2 quadrats). If scoring these is rapid and more ground is covered, however, such a sample size is reasonable.

Continuously distributed data can also be worthwhile and are customarily analyzed using more conventional parametric techniques. Exploratory data analyses typically begin by checking distributions and this is appropriate for browsing measures as well. Such distributions can be sensitively compared using non-parametric techniques like the Kolmogorov-Smirnoff test. When using parametric methods of analysis, we should also check residuals to ensure that these are normally distributed. We can use, for example, t-tests for testing pairs of times or locations and ANOVA for comparing multiple means. As monitoring is continued, it makes sense to apply repeated measures ANOVA.

Analyzing data from exclosures will often be based on paired comparisons including contingency table analyses for discrete dependent variables and paired t-tests for continuously distributed ones. Such in vs. outside comparisons are simple but should be interpreted with caution (see Section 4.5 above). Alternative explanations should also be kept in mind like missing seed banks and the potential that hare browse might account for any differences found (if these are also excluded by the fencing).

Historical vs. Contemporary Data

When interpreting any data from a browse monitoring program, researchers should also bear in mind the historical and geographic context. Historical data even of a qualitative kind are of particular value as they provide a basis for comparison and a benchmark for evaluating current conditions. They address the 'missing baseline' problem allowing a more complete understanding of how browse impacts may have developed over time and just how severe these are relative to historical conditions. Such baselines are rarely detailed and complete, however, leaving us with the question of what is 'normal' or within the range of historical variation?

As data from a browse monitoring program accumulates, we will gradually accumulate a more complete picture of how browsing impacts vary over space and time. Such results are valuable both for the picture they provide of the dynamic ecosystems we are attempting to manage and because knowing such variation and associated error statistics will allow us to improve our monitoring program. Indeed, by analogy with the idea of 'adaptive management' we will increasingly have the opportunity to engage in 'adaptive monitoring.' Eventually, it will also be possible to detect trends and to examine how these develop geographically and over time. As no extensive browsing monitoring scheme yet exists, it is difficult to envision just what these patterns may be or how they might best be analyzed. A related issue concerns our ability to identify 'early warning signs' of impending increases in browsing impacts. Here, having a time series of data on tree seedling and sapling demography and tracking population dynamics and grazing rates on sensitive herbaceous species should be of particular value. We may also be able to devise 'negative' indicators of browse based on increases in growth or dominance by species that tolerate or resist browsing (like hay-scented fern in the eastern U.S. – de la Cretaz and Kelty 1999; de la Cretaz 2002).

Single Species vs. Community / Composite Indicators

As noted above, previous approaches to monitoring ungulate impacts have tended to focus, naturally enough, on the particular plant species they usually eat. For woody plants, these include single species browse indices (like those developed regionally for yew and sugar maple) as well as counts of seedlings and saplings of species known to be sensitive to browsing (like hemlock and northern white cedar). For herbaceous plants, single-species approaches have usually focused on the number, size and/or reproductive condition of particular indicator species like *Trillium* and *Clintonia*. Such indicators have several virtues including that they are:

- justifiable,
- easy to implement (requiring minimal training), and
- usually straightforward to interpret

Alone, however, individual indices of this kind also have some disadvantages. These include that they:

- depend on the plant being present
- may be sensitive to plant density and/or other local conditions
- may have high levels of local variation (inflating sampling variance)
- do not cover a complete range of ungulate impacts

- may be slow to recover from past browsing with recovery dynamics depending on shade, the availability of local seed sources, intrinsic growth rates of each species, and other local factors.

The limitations of single-species indicators of browsing have led several investigators (and us) to further consider how these single-species metrics might be combined, as well as the potential for multi-species indicators based on community composition and structure, i.e., the entire ensemble of woody and/or non-woody plants present at a site. Such multi-species approaches have the potential to:
- respond to browsing impacts across a broader range of ungulate densities by using any and all species present at each site
- include more relevant data, providing more power and reducing error variances (once calibrated)
- provide 'early warning' of impending broader impacts (via changes in the most sensitive species)
- assess transient recovery dynamics by comparing responses of species with faster and slower responses to browsing and by monitoring shifts in the relative abundance of browse-sensitive and browse-tolerant / resistant species

We feel that particular ensemble indicators should be considered for use in the Vital Signs monitoring program as we have strong incentives to develop monitoring techniques that efficiently make use of all data available from as many species as possible.

The community and composite indicators discussed in Section 4.4 are based on both direct measures (like overall levels of browsing among the woody plants present at a site) and indirect measures (like a community's overall species composition and/or patterns of relative abundance). Such pluralistic approaches add statistical power by taking advantage of all species and age/size classes present. However, we still lack a full understanding of how these variables respond to the transient short-term and longer-term impacts of ungulate browsing. We also have yet to cross-calibrate the data generated by these various indicators to compare their reliability and power, and to see which particular composite statistics might prove most useful for assessing browsing impacts. Such steps are needed to extend these methods to our region, and to ensure that they fit the current and future needs of the Vital Signs program.

The particular multi-species composite indicator for woody species that we feel has considerable potential to address the needs of the Vital Signs program is the Morellet Browsing Index (Morellet et al. 2001, 2003). This index scores the presence or absence of available woody twigs in each quadrat and, if present, any browse on those. Although developed in Europe, this index is generalizable, both in being based on all the woody browse present within the 'molar zone' and in terms of its clear and straightforward statistical properties. Because it is simple and unambiguous to score the presence of woody plants and browsing on most species, the BI offers a consistent measure that does not vary much over observers. Its well-understood statistical properties allow the ready calculation of error bars, facilitating comparisons of BI over sites and years. In addition, because it relies on a Bayesian model, one can use previous estimates of BI as the priors for new estimates, potentially improving estimates as time goes on.

Although the Morellet BI was highly correlated with variation in the abundance of roe deer in a forest in S France between 1992-97, this relationship may not always be linear. As noted above, deer impacts tend to vary with the availability of woody browse, its species composition, and past browsing rates. However, as monitoring is continued over time, we should be able to test and eventually account for some of these effects that depend on the local and historical context. For example, the n_p data collected provides a ready measure of woody browse availability. Although Morellet do not explore the idea, one could examine relationships between BI and n_p over sites and over time to test how browsing rates vary with the availability of browse and the past history of browsing. This could further improve the value of BI for predicting impacts on woody plants.

Although the overall BI is based on all woody species present in the sampled quadrats, Morellet et al. (2001, 2003) suggest that species that are problematic to score reliably should be omitted. In addition, if species are distinguished during sampling, it is also possible to test whether browsing rates on different species are independent of each other over quadrats. They found highly significant positive (synergistic) associations between the rates of browsing for several key browse species, suggesting a contagious pattern of browsing in roe deer in quadrats with favored species. A similar contagion was noted by de Knegt et al. (2008). This may help to explain the high variance in browsing observed over quadrats and individuals (e.g. with the sugar maple browse index).

Given this high variance, it is important to sample adequately to obtain reliable estimates to monitor over time. Morellet et al. (2003) evaluated the effects of variable quadrat size and number. Ideally, quadrats should be of a size that has a reasonable probability of including available woody species (so fewer empty plots are sampled). At the same time, they should not be so large that they 'saturate' in terms of having too high a probability that an available plant will be browsed. Based on their results, they recommend a sample of 150 quadrats of 1 m^2 each at each site. Although this sounds like a large sample, the simple nature of the binary scoring makes this work easy to teach and potentially rapid, particularly if the species are not being identified (though that would limit one's ability to do some of the analyses discussed above).

Given the utility of preliminary data (for the prior) and the need to check the proportions of quadrats with woody browse present and with active browse, we recommend doing preliminary surveys at 2-3 forest sites in each Park using perhaps 40-50 quadrats of 4 m^2 each, scoring all four 1 m^2 sub-quadrat separately. This would allow an analysis of which quadrat size (1, 2, or 4 m^2) was best and would provide estimates based on a 200 m^2 sample of woody plant incidence and browse. Further statistical consultation and analyses could allow the GLKN to customize sample sizes and/or spacing and to assess the overall statistical power of this technique in our region.

It is also worthwhile to consider just how sampling for this browse index might be combined with the vegetation sampling planned for the Parks. If, for example, the vegetation sampling called for surveys of 80 spaced 1 m^2 quadrats at each site, surveying the same quadrats plus just one additional one near each of these points would provide a browse sample of 160 quadrats (and 160 m^2). If 2 or 4 m^2 quadrats emerge as ideal based on the preliminary survey recommended above, these could be placed directly on each of 40 or 80 vegetation sampling points, adding very little time to the existing field data surveys. If sampling time permits, we also recommend scoring the number and identity of all tree seedlings and saplings (from 30-300 cm in height) in the basic set (of 40-80) vegetation quadrats. This would provide a secondary metric useful for assessing demographic structure and thus incipient impacts (early warning) or recovery.

For herbaceous species, we also see virtues in combining data from many species into single metrics or indices of deer impacts. Most simply, this would consist of scoring the number, browse condition, and perhaps height of all indicator species known to be sensitive to deer herbivory (lilies, orchids, etc.). Again, this could be done directly in conjunction with the routine vegetation monitoring program, scoring deer damage on plants occurring in the quadrats being sampled anyway. The community data obtained from repeated surveys should be further analyzed to obtain data on changes in the density, structure, and composition of these communities under the assumption that deer browsing may be major contributor to such changes. This assumption should be tested, of course, both by comparing changes in local plant communities to the local woody browse data and by analyzing which species are shifting in abundance. If species known to tolerate and resist browsing are increasing and those known to be palatable and preferred are decreasing, it is usually safe to infer that deer herbivory is a factor. Although such ratings as to deer palatability have usually only been available for a few species in the past (usually based on 'cafeteria' preference trials or observations), the Waller group is currently analyzing a broad suite of functional traits for many of the region's herbaceous plants that should allow us to predict each species' probable suitability as deer food as well as its vulnerability (based on life-history characteristics).

It may also prove possible to infer deer impacts (again, via cross-calibration with the other techniques described above) based on overall changes in community composition. These changes can be described in terms of a vector in multi-dimensional species space where position of the community is represented by both the composition and relative abundance of all species (a technique referred to as ordination). Again, knowing the relative palatability and resistance / tolerance to deer herbivory may allow us to extract a browse axis within this space and then to track movements of local plant communities along this axis.

Discussion and Conclusions

The Significance of Monitoring Ungulate Impacts

Ungulates clearly have a wide-ranging set of impacts on forest plant communities (Section 3). These impacts can also be dramatic not only in terms of affecting woody and non-woody species known to be sensitive to ungulate browsing but also by affecting so many other species at several trophic levels. These impacts extend to ecological processes like exotic invasions, nutrient cycling, and possibly pollination and dispersal services and carbon sequestration. Given this range, diversity, and significance of impacts, we have strong incentives to expand the scope of our efforts to monitor ungulate browsing impacts. Developing an effective and efficient browse monitoring program, however, presents us with a broad menu of choices. Making these choices is hard because we have only limited data for making the right decisions.

A theme in this report has been that efforts to monitor ungulate browsing should initially take a pluralistic research approach by initially considering several alternative methods of gauging browse impacts. A project designed to compare the efficiency, productivity, and reliability of methods in two or more field locations would yield several long-term benefits including estimates of field times required, a chance to judge compatibility with existing vegetation monitoring protocols, statistical comparisons of the techniques including power analyses, and estimation of likely error variances (and thus the precision with which we can estimate various variables). In addition, this project could assess how many data useful for inferring impacts could be garnered from the raw vegetation monitoring data and the efficiency / utility of using these variables (primarily on plant community composition) relative to field estimates of browsing on woody and non-woody plants.

The impact of ungulate browse in ecosystems is a topic of great concern at Great Lakes Network parks. Parks and park managers are charged with maintaining healthy, high functioning ecosystems with high biotic integrity. As such, the high levels of browse have spurred park biologists to develop an understanding of the breadth of the problem. The impacts of deer vary greatly, however, across the nine Network parks. Deer impacts on ecosystems tend to be greater at the more southern Network parks, especially at Indiana Dunes National Lakeshore. Higher edge to forest ratio, fewer natural predators, and possible reduced hunting pressure by humans at the southern parks contribute to this. Nonetheless, northern Network parks are also faced with ungulate browse problems. Many northern parks are, or include, islands on which deer have been absent until recently. In the absence of browse pressure, native plants, including yew (*Taxus canadensis*) are present in greater abundance and size than elsewhere in the region. The establishment of deer on these islands has spurred park biologists to monitor their impacts. Currently, however, monitoring efforts vary greatly between parks, and are often directed at specific and obvious impacts. While these monitoring programs are valuable, they are often not applicable to large areas of the rest of the park, and certainly not between parks. In addition, they are initiated in response to obvious browse impacts.

Subtle shifts in plant communities are occurring regionally. These changes include higher percentages of non-biotically pollinated plants and greater homogenization across large areas. These shifts in community composition may not be immediately evident to park managers because of their subtle nature. Implementation of a broadly-applicable browse protocol should be valuable and, over time, provide parks with a baseline on which to make management decisions.

What's Normal? Assessing Significant Impacts

In designing and implementing ungulate impact monitoring programs, we should strive to construct indices and indicators that will allow us to distinguish between local and regional effects and between short-term and long-term effects. That is, in addition to the statistical fluctuations that represent sampling error, we also encounter variation in field data that reflects the 'noise' in natural systems due to fluctuations in seasonal and annual climate, patchy local disturbance, irregular grouping and movements of ungulates, and sometimes cyclic patterns in regeneration or population density. Detecting regional differences and more consistent trends requires us to screen out enough of this noise to track these more systematic signals.

The most obvious way to do this is to design a monitoring system that is broad enough in geographic extent (and intensive enough within that range) to span spatial variation in ungulate density, vegetative conditions, and associated ungulate impacts. Having identical or similar monitoring methods replicated across several Parks in the region (and, ideally, other ownerships) to span this variation gives us a set of 'natural experiments' for tracking how deer impacts vary with respect to the landscape conditions that surround Parks (Diamond 1983). By the same argument, ungulate monitoring should occur at regular intervals and be extended over enough time to establish clear baselines for the different Parks. Without these baselines, we have no basis for inferring shifts in ungulate impacts which might trigger management responses (Magnuson 1990). Once a monitoring program is in place, the value of the data it generates will correspondingly increase over time and in proportion to the geographic extent of that (or similar) sampling.

Extended and extensive monitoring is particularly important for tracking ungulate impacts in that these are often cumulative in nature and long-lasting in terms of their effects on natural systems. We also lack good data on rates of recovery from these impacts and how these, too, may depend on landscape context. Over time, however, we will gain these data, allowing us to estimate the severity and potential for recovery from browse impacts in advance. For example, if ungulates radically alter competitive dominance relationships among browse tolerant species, and these competitive differences are sustained or amplified over time, we may need to be alert and wary about growing deer impacts. That is, if ungulate impacts in Upper Great Lakes forests are strongly cumulative and difficult to reverse (as it appears to be in some tropical savannas – Sternberg 2001), we may need to monitor impacts quite closely and respond as soon as incipient major impacts become evident. If, on the other hand, such 'hysteresis' is uncommon in these forests, there may be more latitude to delay responses, or respond more modestly to evidence of growing ungulate impacts. A sustained monitoring system will give the understanding we need to anticipate the consequences of current actions (or inaction) and thus to know whether radical or more modest management responses are more appropriate.

Values of Various Kinds of Data

As already noted, fenced **exclosures** are of particular value for monitoring ungulate impacts for several reasons. a) They provide direct evidence of ungulate impacts in a controlled experimental setting. b) Such exclosures can be placed to evaluate ungulate impacts on particular species or in particular areas and to assess how these accumulate over time. c) They can provide visually arresting demonstrations of ungulate impacts with great educational value. However, exclosures can also inflate impressions of ungulate effects by creating extreme comparisons to an artificial zero-browsing baseline. To be most useful, exclosures should be replicated and maintained to allow detailed comparisons of community responses over time as explained above. Placing exclosures in proximity to trails and/or visitor centers would enhance their educational value but might underestimate ungulate impacts if human traffic deterred ungulate use of these areas.

We have developed and promoted in this Report the notion that a pluralistic or synthetic approach to monitoring ungulate impacts makes sense. Traditional single-species indicators include the presence, size, and flowering conditions of particular species known to be sensitive to ungulate browsing. Whenever such species are encountered in routine vegetation surveys, it makes sense to note these variables as it takes little extra field time or expertise. It has also been popular to record the incidence of ungulate browse on single woody species in the past (e.g., the sugar maple browse index – Frelich and Lorimer 1985). We are less enthusiastic about relying on such individual species measures of woody browsing given the deficiencies noted earlier. Nevertheless, we recommend noting species when scoring browsed and unbrowsed species for composite indicators (like Morellet et al.'s Browsing Index) provided this can be done economically and reliably (i.e., if the field team scoring browse is confident in their woody plant identification skills). Having such data in hand would allow one to track shifts in the woody plant composition of the 'molar zone' as well as shifts in the relative rates of browsing among species over time and space. The Morellet index is itself, then, a broadly applicable synthetic index of the kind we advocate.

Integration with Vegetation Monitoring

We are also cautiously optimistic about the potential value of other synthetic indicators that make use of the understory plant community data generated from the vegetation monitoring program. Given that these data are being generated anyway, it makes sense to assess their value for monitoring deer impacts by analyzing relationships with more conventional indicators including the herbaceous indicators noted above, any woody browsing index available, and data from fenced exclosures. Our hope is that such plant community indicators could provide data that will complement and reinforce the power of the other kinds of data available to provide a fuller picture of ungulate impacts. The broad set of plants present in forest understories express various sensitivities to deer herbivory and differential rates of recovery from herbivory. Thus, it seems likely that information on their absolute and relative abundance (and possibly their size and cover) could be used to construct a composite indicator, or set of composite indicators, of ungulate impacts. If, for example, species disappear from the community in a more or less predictable order, we should be able to use the composition of the community to infer the severity of herbivory.

A composite index of ungulate browse might then be generated via multivariate analyses of the understory community composition as discussed in Section 4.4. Such an index would presumably reflect some kind of weighted average of current and past herbivory. It might also prove possible, over time and with experience, to relate shifts in the abundance (or relative abundance) of species within the community to transient increases or decreases in herbivory. Likewise, the demographic (size) structure of tree seedlings might also provide a sensitive 'early warning' of incipient changes in deer herbivory with implications for forest structure.

We clearly stand to gain efficiency by combining field studies of ungulate impacts with the routine vegetation monitoring program planned for Parks in the region (Sanders et al. 2008; Johnson et al. 2008). Travel time and the time to locate and lay out sites for monitoring are both appreciable, as is the time invested in the vegetation surveys themselves. Any inferences regarding ungulate impacts made from the vegetation survey data themselves clearly cost no extra field time or effort (though time to analyze, interpret, and distribute the results would still be needed). This efficiency extends to include the time saved by sharing data entry and checking and potentially shared subsequent analyses.

However, we cannot yet rely only on routine vegetation data to infer browse impacts as these metrics have yet to be developed. Developing them depends on having further independent data (e.g. on woody browse and/or exclosures). Once they are developed, we may also learn that these additional data are needed to continuously re-calibrate them and enhance their value. For these reasons, we recommend that ungulate monitoring programs spend an initial period of 6-10 years developing and testing a combination of indicators like those discussed here.

Ways to Maximize Statistical Power

Many established monitoring programs use inadequate sample sizes and thus collect data that cannot be used reliably to detect changes over time in the measured response variables (Legg and Nagy 2006). These monitoring programs run the risk of not promptly warning resource managers and the public of immanent threats to monitored resources (Peterman 1990). The probability of detecting a true change in a given sample is referred to as '**power**' (Sokal and Rohlf 1995), a statistical concept that is influenced by the variance in parameter estimates, the *type I error rate* (the probability of detecting a false change), and the *effect size* (the change observed). High statistical power is desired in any serious monitoring program, and there are a few ways to achieve this.

The most appealing way to gain higher power is to increase sample sizes both within and among sites so as to produce parameter estimates with smaller variances capable of detecting smaller differences. As we suggested to the Park Service in an earlier technical report (Johnson et al. 2006), sampling more intensively within sites is more efficient than sampling a larger number of sites, given the travel time required to reach new sites. It is, however, also important that enough sites be sampled to adequately represent the habitats being monitored among parks. Sites to be sampled have already been selected by the GLKN for the vegetation monitoring program (Sanders et al. 2008). We propose that these same sites be used to monitor deer impacts.

All too often resource managers must reign in sample sizes to meet their limited budgets. Given this reality, we can also consider other approaches for increasing power, including decreasing the acceptable rate of false negatives in lieu of a higher rate of false positives (i.e., 0.1 alpha instead of the standard 0.05 alpha). Small effect sizes are often difficult to detect, so increasing the detectable level of change is also an option (Elzinga et al. 1998), as is applying more powerful statistical analyses such as one-sided tests.

Indicator species have long been used by resource managers to track ecological changes (e.g., Cairns 1986; Landres et al. 1988; Noss 1990; Crow et al. 1994). The skewed nature of plant community data, with only a few species being common and the majority being rare or absent (McCune and Grace 2002), results in only a handful of species being abundant enough to serve as indicator species that return data with enough power to detect change. Johnson et al. (2007) conducted a priori power analyses on vegetation monitoring methods being considered by the GLKN; they determined that the majority of all indicators at the species level did not return high enough power to detect 20% changes in a suite of response variables measured. Hence, as proposed here, we support the use of *composite indicators* to track ungulate impacts on plant communities within and among the GLKN parks.

We also advocate using multiple indicators to increase the probability that deer impacts will be detected soon enough to be useful in adjusting management. Strong indicators of deer impacts in one habitat or park may not serve to detect changes in other areas. For example, Johnson et al.'s (2006, 2008) power analyses determined that a 20% change in the density of shrub stems (using the Forest Inventory and Analysis plot design) could be detected in Apostle Islands National Lakeshore, but not among sites sampled with the same intensity in Pictured Rocks National Lakeshore.

Several types of data can and should be used to infer the impacts of deer on plant communities in the Great Lakes Network parks. In particular, we propose that the GLKN collect data on woody browse, understory community composition and structure, and the size and condition of any indicator species present at the sites already being monitored for vegetation change. For simplicity and the ability to compare data over parks and over time, we favor using the Morellet Browsing Index (Morellet et al. 2001, 2003) based on scoring the presence/absence of available woody vegetation and the presence/absence of browsed twigs within fixed-size plots. To assess the influence of browsing on the herbaceous community, we have proposed here that a few measurements be made on a set of indicator species likely to be encountered by botanists scoring quadrats for the presence/absence of all groundlayer species for the vegetation monitoring program.

These additional measurements should include: number of individuals, presence/absence of deer browsing (i.e., removal of flowering scapes or leaves), and the maximum height of each indicator species. The plant community data already being collected by the vegetation monitoring program may also provide insights on the influences of deer within and among sites throughout the GLKN parks. The value of these plant community data become more valuable when combined with a database of plant functional traits including information on the relative palatability (e.g., fiber content, in vitro digestibility, nutrient contents) and tolerance (e.g., resprouting ability and growth form) to repeated browsing by deer.

Elements of a Suggested Monitoring Program for Upper Great Lakes Parks

Opportunity. Ungulate browsing represents both a key ecological process in the National Park units in the Upper Great Lakes region and a significant threat to plant and animal abundance and diversity in many of those units. The NPS GLKN thus has a responsibility to design and implement a comprehensive and sustained monitoring program on ungulate impacts. The great variation that exists across the region among Park units in ungulate impacts (and accompanying variation within several units) further creates a special opportunity for detecting, understanding, and responding to the threats posed by ungulate browsing.

Design. In embarking on a systematic program to monitor ungulate impacts, the NPS GLKN should incorporate a contemporary understanding of the relevant variables to monitor, adequate sampling to provide statistical power, the use of data from several complementary indicators, and regular reviews to evaluate how the program might be modified to make it more efficient and effective. In the interest in advancing this design, we make the following specific suggestions.

Herbaceous Indicator Species. The first element in a program efficiently designed to assess the impacts of ungulate browsing would be to extend the data generated by the existing vegetative monitoring program to include taking note of the height and any conspicuous browse damage to vegetative and reproductive stems on particular species present and likely to be informative (as noted in Sections 4.2 and 4.3).
Woody Browse Index. To complement data from monitoring particular herbaceous species known to be palatable to deer, we also recommend that browsing on woody plants present in the browsing zone be monitored at the sites where vegetative monitoring is occurring. This monitoring should note both the woody browse present and available and the incidence of browsing on those plants. For efficiency and simplicity, these data should be scored in simple terms (e.g., as binary variables within many replicated small sampling plots).

Composite community indicators. To complement data from specific herbaceous and woody indicators like those suggested above, we further suggest making use of the data on plant species abundances and community composition generated by the vegetation monitoring program. Analyses of these data and comparisons with other indicators available could allow creation of a composite indicator (perhaps customized by Park unit) capable of detecting browse impacts in terms of trends in community composition and/or density and stature. Such composite indicators might allow us to detect and respond to ungulate impacts across a wide range of browsing intensities and histories.

Exclosures. To complement more passive indicators, we strongly suggest that Park units also seek resources to establish, maintain and monitor replicate fenced exclosures within or near their boundaries. Such exclosures would provide experimental rigor for detecting ongoing (though not previous) ungulate impacts and for monitoring the nature and rates of recovery possible if ungulate browsing were reduced. Smaller, localized exclosures could also provide a management tool for protecting particular rare plant individuals or populations. Finally, if such exclosures were located along trails or near other frequently visited sites, they could contribute to public education and public support for any needed ungulate control programs.

Adaptive monitoring and management cycles. Because the several different suggested indicators yield different kinds of data, not all of which have been tested and confirmed as useful, there is a need to evaluate, compare, and cross-calibrate the metrics generated from the indicators outlined above. Engaging in regular reviews and evaluations of these data and metrics will allow opportunities to adjust the monitoring methods, the data collected, and/or methods of analysis to improve their utility and to make maximum use of the knowledge being gained. In addition, the goal in collecting and analyzing these data is to generate enough understanding of ungulate impacts to adjust management

Partnerships. There may be opportunities to partner with state and other federal agencies in the region to develop and implement such a comprehensive and sustained 'adaptive monitoring' program. Such monitoring would reap many rewards over the years including a fuller understanding of ungulate – plant community interactions and greater public support for ungulate management efforts.

Literature Cited

Allison, T. D. 1990a. The influence of deer browsing on the reproductive biology of Canada yew (*Taxus canadensis* marsh.). I. Direct effect on pollen, ovule, and seed production. Oecologia **83**:523-529.

Allison, T. D. 1990b. The influence of deer browsing on the reproductive biology of Canada yew (*Taxus canadensis* marsh.). II. Pollen limitation: an indirect effect. Oecologia **83**:530-534.

Allombert, S., A. J. Gaston, and J-L. Martin. 2005a. A natural experiment on the impact of overabundant deer on songbird populations. Biological Conservation **126**:1-13.

Allombert, S., S. Stockton, and J.-L. Martin. 2005b. A natural experiment on the impact of overabundant deer on forest invertebrates. Conservation Biology **19**:1917-1929.

Alverson, W. S. and D. M. Waller. 1997. Deer populations and the widespread failure of hemlock regeneration in northern forests. Pages 280–297 *in* W. McShea and J. Rappole (eds.), The Science of Overabundance: Deer Ecology and Population Management. Smithsonian Institution Press, Washington, D.C.

Anderson, R. C. 1994. Height of white-flowered trillium (*Trillium grandiflorum*) as an index of deer browsing intensity. Ecological Applications **4**:104-109.

Anderson, R. C., and A. J. Katz. 1993. Recovery of browse-sensitive tree species following release from white-tailed deer (*Odocoileus virginianus* Zimmerman) browsing pressure. Biological Conservation **63**:203-208.

Anderson, R. C., and O. L. Loucks. 1979. White-tail deer (*Odocoileus virginianus*) influence on the structure and composition of *Tsuga canadensis* forests. Journal of Applied Ecology **16**:855-861.

Augustine, D. J., and D. DeCalesta. 2003. Defining deer overabundance and threats to forest communities: from individual plants to landscape structure. Ecoscience **10**:472-486.

Augustine, D. J., and L. E. Frelich. 1998. Effects of white-tailed deer on populations of an understory forb in fragmented deciduous forests. Conservation Biology **12**:995-1004.

Augustine, D. J., L. E. Frelich, and P. A. Jordan. 1998. Evidence for two alternative stable states in an ungulate grazing system. Ecological Applications **8**:1260-1269.

Augustine, D. J., and S. J. McNaughton. 1998. Ungulate effects on the functional species composition of plant communities: herbivore selectivity and plant tolerance. Journal of Wildlife Management **62**:1165-1183.

Balgooyen, C. P., and D. M. Waller. 1995. The use of *Clintonia borealis* and other indicators to gauge impacts of white-tailed deer on plant communities in northern Wisconsin, USA. Natural Areas Journal **15**:308-318.

Batcheler, C. L. 1975. Development of a distance method for deer census using pellet groups. Journal of Wildlife Management **39**:641-652.

Beals, E. W., G. Cottam, and R. G. Vogel. 1960. Influence of deer on the vegetation of the Apostle Islands, Wisconsin. Journal of Wildlife Management **24**:68-80.

Bennett, L. J., P. F. English, and R. McCain. 1940. A study of deer populations by use of pellet-group counts. Journal of Wildlife Management **4**:398-403.

Binkley, D., M. M. Moore, and W. H. Romme. 2006. Was Aldo Leopold right about the Kaibab deer herd? Ecosystems **9**:227-241.

Blewett, T. J. 1976. Structure and dynamics of the McDougall Springs lowland forest. M.S. Department of Botany, University of Wisconsin - Madison.

Brandner, T. A., R. O. Peterson, and K. L. Risenhoover. 1990. Balsam fir on Isle Royale: effects of moose herbivory and population density. Ecology **71**:155-164.

Brewer, R. 1980. A half-century of changes in the herb layer of a climax deciduous forest in Michigan. Journal of Ecology **68**:823-832.

Cairns, J. 1986. The myth of the most sensitive species. BioScience **36**:670-672.

Callaway, R. M., and W. M. Ridenour. 2004. Novel weapons: invasive success and the evolution of increased competitive ability. Frontiers in Ecology and the Environment **2**:436-443.

Carpenter, S., J. F. Kitchell, J. R. Hodgson, P. A. Cochran, J. J. Elser, M. M. Elser, and D. M. Lodge. 1987. Regulation of lake primary productivity by food web structure. Ecology **68**:1863-1876.

Caughley, G. 1970. Eruption of ungulate populations, with special emphasis on Himalayan thar of New Zealand. Ecology **51**:53-72.

Caughley, G. 1983. The deer wars: the story of deer in New Zealand. Heinemann Publishers, Auckland.

Cingolani, A. M., G. Posse, and M. B. Collantes. 2005. Plant functional traits, herbivore selectivity and response to sheep grazing in Patagonian steppe grasslands. Journal of Applied Ecology **42**:50-59.

Cote, M., J. Ferron, and R. Gagnon. 2003. Impact of seed and seedling predation by small rodents on early regeneration establishment of black spruce. Canadian Journal of Forest Research **33**:2362-2371.

Côté, S. D., T. P. Rooney, J-P. Tremblay, C. Dussault, and D. M. Waller. 2004. Ecological impacts of deer overabundance. Annual Review of Ecology, Evolution, and Systematics **35**:113-147.

Crête, M. 1999. The distribution of deer biomass in North America supports the hypothesis of exploitation ecosystems. Ecology Letters **2**:223-227.

Crow, T. R., A. Haney, and D. M. Waller. 1994. Report on the scientific roundtable on biological diversity convened by the Chequamegon and Nicolet National Forests. General Technical Report NC-166, USDA Forest Service, North Central Forest Experiment Station, St. Paul.

Davidson, D. W. 1993. The effects of herbivory and granivory on terrestrial plant succession. Oikos **68**:23-35.

Davis, M. B., T. E. Parshall, and J. B. Ferrari. 1996. Landscape heterogeneity of hemlock-hardwood forest in northern Michigan. Pages 291-304 *in* M. B. Davis, editor. Northeastern Old-Growth Forest. Island Press, Washington, DC.

deCalesta, D. S. 1994. Effect of white-tailed deer on songbirds within managed forests in Pennsylvania. Journal of Wildlife Management. **58**:711-717.

deCalesta, D. S., and S. L. Stout. 1997. Relative deer density and sustainability: a conceptual framework for integrating deer management with ecosystem management. Wildlife Society Bulletin **25**:252-258.

de Knegt, H. J., T. A. Groen, C. A. D. M. v. d. Vijver, H. H. T. Prins, and F. v. Langevelde. 2008. Herbivores as architects of savannas: inducing and modifying spatial vegetation patterning. Oikos **117**:543-554.

de la Cretaz, A. 2002. Development of tree regeneration in fern-dominated forest understories after reduction of deer browsing. Restoration Ecology **10**:416-426.

de la Cretaz, A., and M. J. Kelty. 1999. Establishment and control of hay-scented fern: a native invasive species. Biological Invasions **1**:223-236.

Diamond, J. M. 1983. Laboratory, field, and natural experiments. Nature **304**:586-587.

Didier, K. A., and W. F. Porter. 2003. Relating spatial patterns of sugar maple reproductive success and relative deer density in northern New York state. Forest Ecology and Management. **181**:253-266.

Elzinga, C. L., D. W. Salzer, and J. W. Willoughby. 1998. Measuring and Monitoring Plant Populations. Bureau of Land Management Technical Reference 1730-1, BLM/RS/ST-98/005+1730.

Eschtruth, A. K., and J. J. Battles. 2008. Acceleration of exotic plant invasion in a forested ecosystem by a generalist herbivore. Conservation Biology **23**:388-399.

Fletcher, J. D., W. J. McShea, L. A. Shipley, and D. Shumway. 2001a. Use of common forest forbs to measure browsing pressure by white-tailed deer (*Odocoileus virginianus* Zimmerman) in Virginia, USA. Natural Areas Journal **21**:172-176.

Fletcher, J. D., L. A. Shipley, W. J. McShea, and D. L. Shumway. 2001b. Wildlife herbivory and rare plants: the effects of white-tailed deer, rodents, and insects on growth and survival of Turk's cap lily. Biological Conservation **101**:229-238.

Flowerdew, J. R., and S. A. Ellwood. 2001. Impacts of woodland deer on small mammal ecology Forestry **74**:277-287.

Frelich, L. E., and C. G. Lorimer. 1985. Current and predicted long-term effects of deer browsing in hemlock forests in Michigan, U.S.A. Biological Conservation **34**:99-120.

Frye, R. 2008. Deer Wars: Science, Tradition, and the Battle over Managing Whitetails in Pennsylvania. Keystone Book, Pennsylvania State Univ. Press, University Park, PA.

Fuller, T. K. 1991. Do pellet counts index white-tailed deer numbers and population change? Journal of Wildlife Management. **55**:393-396.

Garrott, R. A., P. J. White, and C. A. V. White. 1993. Overabundance: an issue for conservation biologists? Conservation Biology **7**:944-949.

George, L. O., and F. A. Bazzaz. 1999. The fern understory as an ecological filter: emergence and establishment of canopy-tree seedlings. Ecology **80**:833-845.

Gilliam, F. S., and M. R. Roberts. 2003. The Herbaceous Layer in Forests of Eastern North America. Pp. 408. Oxford Univ. Press, New York.

Graham, S. A. 1954. Changes in northern Michigan's forests from browsing by deer. Trans. 19th N. Amer. Wildlife Conf. **19**:526-533.

Guibert, B. 1997. Une nouvelle approche des populations de chevreuils en forét: l'Indice de pression sur la flore. Bulletin Technique ONF **32**:5-13.

Hartley, S. E., and C. G. Jones. 1997. Plant Chemistry and Herbivory, or Why the World is Green. Pages 284-324 *in* M. J. Crawley, editor. Plant Ecology. Blackwell Science Ltd. , Oxford, Great Britain.

Heckel, C. D., and S. Kalisz. 2008. Generalist herbivores drive unpalatable species decline: Collateral damage of abundant ungulate browsers. *Meeting Abstract*. Ecological Society of America, http://eco.confex.com/eco/2008/techprogram/P14739.HTM.

Hester, A. J., L. Edenius, R. M. Buttenschon, and A. T. Kuiters. 2000. Interactions between forests and herbivores: the role of controlled grazing experiments. Forestry **73**:381-391.

Hobbs, N. T. 1996. Modification of ecosystems by ungulates. Journal of Wildlife Management **60**:695-713.

Horsley, S. B., S. L. Stout, and D. S. DeCalesta. 2003. White-tailed deer impact on the vegetation dynamics of a northern hardwood forest. Ecological Applications **13**:98-118.

Inouye, R. S., T. D. Allison, and N. C. Johnson. 1994. Old field succession on a Minnesota sand plain: effects of deer and other factors on invasion by trees. Bulletin of the Torrey Botanical Club **121**:266-276.

Janzen, D. H. 1983. No park is an island: increase in interference from the outside as park size decreases. Oikos **41**:402-410.

Johnson, A. S., P. E. Hale, W. M. Ford, J. M. Wentworth, J. R. French, O. F. Anderson, and G. B. Pullen. 1995. White-tailed deer foraging in relation to successional stage, overstory type, and management of southern Appalachian forests. American Midland Naturalist **133**:18-35.

Johnson, A. S., P. E. Hale, W. M. Ford, J. M. Wentworth, J. R. French, O. F. Anderson, and G. B. Pullen. 1995. White-tailed deer foraging in relation to successional stage, overstory type, and management of southern Appalachian forests. American Midland Naturalist **133**:18-35.

Johnson, S.E., Mudrak, E.L., and Waller, D.M. 2006. A comparison of sampling methodologies for long-term monitoring in the Great Lakes Network National Parks. National Park Service, Great Lakes Inventory and Monitoring Network Report: GLKN/2006/3. 140 pp.

Johnson, S. E., E. L. Mudrak, and D. M. Waller. 2008. Comparing power among three sampling methods for monitoring forest vegetation. Canadian Journal of Forest Research **38**:143-156.

Jones, T. 2008. Moose are roaming right out of existence: In the upper Midwest, the animals are dying off in startling numbers. Biologists blame global warming. *in* Los Angeles Times, Los Angeles, CA.

Jordan, P. A., R. O. Peterson, J. P. Campbell, and B. McLaren. 1993. Comparison of pellet counts and aerial counts for estimating density of moose at Isle Royale: a progress report. Alces **29**:267-278.

Judziewicz, E. J., and R. G. Koch. 1993. Flora and vegetation of the Apostle Islands National Lakeshore and Madeline Island, Ashland and Bayfield Counties, Wisconsin. Michigan Botanist **32**:43-189.

Karr, J. R., M. Dionne, and I. Schlosser. 1992. Bottom-up versus top-down regulation of vertebrate populations: lessons from birds and fish. Pages 244-286 *in* M. D. Hunter, T. Ohgushi, and P. W. Price, editors. Effects of Resource Distribution on Animal-Plant Interactions. Academic Press, New York.

Kirschbaum, C. D., and B. L. Anacker. 2005. The utility of *Trillium* and *Maianthemum* as phyto-indicators of deer impact in northwestern Pennsylvania, USA. Forest Ecology and Management. **217**:54-66.

Kitterage, D. B., P. Mark, and S. Ashton. 1995. Impact of deer browsing on regeneration in mixed stands in southern New England. Northern Journal of Applied Forestry. **12**:115-120.

Kraft, L. S., T. R. Crow, D. S. Buckley, E. Z. Nauertz, and J. C. Zasada. 2004. Effects of harvesting and deer browsing on attributes of understory plants in northern hardwood forests, Upper Michigan, USA. Forest Ecology and Management. **199**:219-230.

Landres, P. B., J. Verner, and J. W. Thomas. 1988. Ecological uses of vertebrate indicator species: a critique. Conservation Biology **2**:316-328.

Langdon, C. 2001. A Comparison of White-Tailed Deer Population Estimation Methods in West Virginia. Pp. 130. Forestry. West Virginia University, Morgantown.

Latham, R., R. Brubaker, M. D. Grund, S. B. Horseley, B. C. Jones, W. H. McWilliams, S. Nicholas, C. K. Nielsen, C. S. Rosenberry, R. S. Seymour, B. P. Shissler, and D.M.Waller. 2008. Monitoring deer impacts in Pennsylvania State Forests. Bureau of Forestry, Pennsylvania Dept. of Conservation & Natural Resources, Harrisburg, PA.

Leach, M. K., and T. J. Givnish. 1996. Ecological determinants of species loss in remnant prairies. Science **273**:1555-1558.

Legg, C.J., and Nagy, L. 2006. Why most conservation monitoring is, but need not be, a waste of time. Journal of Environmental Management **78**:194-199.

Leopold, A. 1933. Game Management. Charles Scribner's Sons, New York.

Leopold, A. 1936. Deer and Dauerwald in Germany I. History. Journal of Forestry **34**:366-375.

Leopold, A. 1943a. The excess deer problem. Audubon **45**:156-157.

Leopold, A. 1943b. Deer irruptions. Transactions of the Wisconsin Academy of Sciences, Arts, and Letters **35**:351–366.

Leopold, A. 1946. The deer dilemma. Wisconsin Conservation Bulletin **11**:3-5.

Leopold, A. 1949. A Sand County Almanac and Sketches Here and There. Oxford Univ. Press, New York.

Magnuson, J. 1990. Long term research and the invisible present. BioScience **40**:495-501.

Martin, J.-L., and C. Baltzinger. 2002. Interactions among deer browse, hunting, and tree regeneration. Canadian Journal of Forest Research **32**:1254-1264.

Mayfield, M. M., D. Ackerly, & G. C. Daily. 2006. The diversity and conservation of plant reproductive and dispersal functional traits in human-dominated tropical landscapes. Journal of Ecology **94**:522-536.

McCabe, R. E., and T. R. McCabe. 1984. Of slings and arrows: An historical retrospective. Pages 19-72 *in* L. K. Halls, editor. White-tailed deer ecology and management. Stackpole Books, Harrisburg, PA.

McCullough, D. R. 1984. Lessons from the George Reserve *in* L. K. Halls, ed. White-tailed deer: Ecology and management. Stackpole Books, Harrisburg, PA.

McCune, B., and J.B. Grace. 2002. Analysis of ecological communities. MjM Software Design, Gleneden Beach, Oregon.

McGraw, J. B., and M. A. Furedi. 2005. Deer browsing and population viability of forest understory plant. Science **307**:920-922.

McLaren, B. E., and R. O. Peterson. 1994. Wolves, moose, and tree rings on Isle Royale. Science **266**:1555-1558.

McNaughton, S. J. 1976. Serengeti migration wildebeest: facilitation of energy flow by grazing. Science **53**:92-94.

McNaughton, S. J. 1985. Ecology of grazing cost : the Serengeti. Ecological Monographs **53**:291-320.

McShea, W. J., and J. H. Rappole. 1997. The science and politics of managing deer within a protected area. Wildlife Society Bulletin **25**:443-446.

McCaffery, K. R., J. Tranetzki, and J. Piechura. 1974. Summer foods of deer in Northern Wisconsin. Journal of Wildlife Management **38**:215-219.

McShea, W. J., and J. H. Rappole. 1997. Herbivores and the Ecology of Forest Understory Birds. Pages 298-309 *in* W. J. McShea, H. B. Underwood, and J. H. Rappole, editors. The Science of Overabundance: Deer Ecology and Population Management. Smithsonian Inst. Press, Washington, D.C.

McShea, W. J., and J. H. Rappole. 2000. Managing the abundance and diversity of breeding bird populations through manipulation of deer populations. Conservation Biology **14**:1161-1170.

McShea, W. J., H. B. Underwood, and J. H. Rappole. 1997. The Science of Overabundance: Deer Ecology and Population Management. Smithsonian Institution Press, Washington, DC.

Michael, E. D. 1992. Impact of deer browsing on regeneration of balsam fir in Canaan Valley, West Virginia. Northern Journal of Applied Forestry **9**:89-90.

Michigan DNR. 2006. Emerging disease issues. URL - http://www.michigan.gov/bovineTB.

Miller, S. G., S. P. Bratton, and J. Hadidian. 1992. Impacts of white-tailed deer on endangered plants. Natural Areas Journal **12**:67-74.

Minnesota DNR. 2005. Status of wildlife populations - Fall, 2005. http://www.dnr.state.mn.us/publications/wildlife/populationstatus2005.html.

Minnesota DNR. 2006. Status of wildlife populations - Fall, 2006. *http://files.dnr.state.mn.us/publications/wildlife/populationstatus2006/populationstatus2006.pdf*

Morellet, N., P. Ballon, Y. Boscardin, and S. Champeley. 2003. A new index to measure roe deer (*Capreolus capreolus*) browsing pressure on woody flora. Game and Wildlife Science **20**:155-173.

Morellet, N., S. Champely, J.-J. Gaillard, P. Ballon, and Y. Boscardin. 2001. The browsing index: new tool uses browsing pressure to monitor deer populations. Wildlife Society Bulletin **29**:1243-1252.

Mudrak, E.L., S.E. Johnson, and D.M. Waller. 2009. Forty-seven year changes in vegetation at the Apostle Islands: Effects of deer on the forest understory In press, Natural Areas Journal.

Myers, J. A., M. Vellend, S. Gardescu, and P. L. Marks. 2004. Seed dispersal by white-tailed deer: implications for long-distance dispersal, invasion, and migration of plants in eastern North America. Oecologia **139**:35-44.

Nelson, M. E., and L. D. Mech. 2006. A 3-decade dearth of deer (*Odocoileus virginianus*) in a wolf (*Canis lupis*)-dominated ecosystem. American Midland Naturalist **155**:373-382.

Noss, R. 1990. Indicators for monitoring biodiversity: A hierarchical approach. Conservation Biology **4**:355-364.

Opperman, J. J., and A. M. Merenlender. 2000. Deer herbivory as an ecological constraint to restoration of degraded riparian corridors. Restoration Ecology **8**:41-47.

Patel, A., and D. J. Rapport. 2000. Assessing the effects of deer browsing, prescribed burns, visitor use, and trails on an oak-pine forest: Pinery Provincial Park, Ontario. Natural Areas Journal **20**:250-260.

Peterman, R.M. 1990. The importance of reporting statistical power: the forest decline and acidic deposition example. Ecology **71**:2024-2027.

Potvin, F., and L. Breton. 2005. From the field: Testing 2 aerial survey techniques on deer in fenced enclosures - visual double-counts and thermal infrared sensing. Wildlife Society Bulletin **33**:317-325.

Potvin, F., L. Breton, and L. P. Rivest. 2002. Testing a double-count aerial survey technique for white-tailed deer, *Odocoileus virginianus*, in Quebec. Canadian Field Naturalist **116**:488-496.

Redford, K. H. 1992. The empty forest. BioScience **42**:412-422.

Ripple, W. J., and R. L. Beschta. 2003. Wolf reintroduction, predation risk, and cottonwood recovery in Yellowstone National Park. Forest Ecology and Management. **184**:299-313.

Ripple, W. J., and R. L. Beschta. 2004a. Wolves and the ecology of fear: Can predation risk structure ecosystems? BioScience **54**:755-766.

Ripple, W. J., and R. L. Beschta. 2004b. Linking wolves and plants: Aldo Leopold on trophic cascades. BioScience **55**:613–621.

Ritchie, M. E., D. Tilman, and J. N. H. Knops. 1998. Herbivore effects on plant and nitrogen dynamics in oak savannah. Ecology **79**:165-177.

Rogers, D. A. 2006. Fifty years of change in southern Wisconsin forests: patterns of species loss and homogenization. PhD thesis, Dept. of Botany. University of Wisconsin, Madison, Wisconsin.

Rooney, T. P. 1997. Escaping herbivory: refuge effects on the morphology and shoot demography of the clonal forest herb, *Maianthemum canadense*. Journal of the Torrey Botanical Society **124**:280-285.

Rooney, T. P. 2001. Impacts of white-tailed deer to forest ecosystems: a North American perspective. Forestry **74**:201-208.

Rooney, T. P., and W. J. Dress. 1997. Species loss over sixty six years in the ground-layer vegetation of Heart's Content, an old growth forest in Pennsylvania, USA. Natural Areas Journal **17**:297-305.

Rooney, T. P., R. J. McCormick, S. L. Solheim, and D. M. Waller. 2000. Regional variation in recruitment of eastern hemlock seedlings in the Southern Superior Uplands Section of the Laurentian Mixed Forest Province, USA. Ecological Applications. **10**:1119-1132.

Rooney, T. P., S. L. Solheim, and D. M. Waller. 2002. Factors influencing the regeneration of northern white cedar in lowland forests of the Upper Great Lakes region, USA. Forest Ecology and Management. **163**:119-130.

Rooney, T. P., and D. M. Waller. 1998. Local and regional variation in hemlock seedling establishment in forests of the upper Great Lakes region, USA. Forest Ecology and Management. **111**:211-224.

Rooney, T. P., and D. M. Waller. 2001. How experimental defoliation and leaf height affect growth and reproduction in *Trillium grandiflorum*. Journal of the Torrey Botanical Society **128**:393-399.

Rooney, T. P., and D. M. Waller. 2003. Direct and indirect effects of deer in forest ecosystems. Forest Ecology and Management. **181**:165-176.

Rooney, T. P., S. M. Wiegmann, D. A. Rogers, and D. M. Waller. 2004. Biotic impoverishment and homogenization in unfragmented forest understory communities. Conservation Biology **18**:787-798.

Ross, B. A., J. R. Bray, and W. H. Marshall. 1970. Effects of long-term deer exclusion on *Pinus resinosa* forest in north-central Minnesota. Ecology **51**:1088-1093

Route, B., and J. Elias (editors). 2005. Draft long-term ecological monitoring plan: Phase III report. U.S. National Park Service, Great Lakes Inventory and Monitoring Network.

Rowland, M. M., G. C. White, and E. M. Karlen. 1984. Use of pellet-group plots to measure trends in deer and elk populations. Wildlife Society Bulletin **12**:147-155.

Roy, V., and S. de Blois. 2006. Using functional traits to assess the role of hedgerow corridors as environmental filters for forest herbs. Biological Conservation **130**:592-603.

Ruhren, S., and M. Dudash. 1996. Consequences of the timing of seed release of *Erythronium americanum* (Liliaceae), a deciduous forest myrmecochore. American Journal of Botany **83**:633-640.

Ruhren, S., and S. L. Handel. 2003. Herbivory constrains survival, reproduction, and mutualisms when restoring nine temperate forest herbs. Journal of the Torrey Botanical Society **130**:34-42.

Ruhren, S., and S. N. Handel. 2000. Considering herbivory, reproduction, and gender when monitoring plants: A case study of Jack-in-the-pulpit (*Arisaema triphyllum* L. Schott). Natural Areas Journal **20**:261-266.

Sanders, S., S. E. Johnson, and D. M. Waller. 2008. Vegetation monitoring protocol: Great Lakes Inventory & Monitoring Network. Natural Resource Report NPS/GLKN/NRR—2008/056. National Park Service, Fort Collins, Colorado.

Shea, K., and P. Chesson. 2002. Community ecology theory as a framework for biological invasions. Trends in Ecology and Evolution **17**:170-176.

Skinner, W. R., and E. S. Telfer. 1974. Spring, summer, and fall foods of deer in New Brunswick. Journal of Wildlife Management **38**:210-214.

Snyder, J. D., and R. A. Janke. 1976. Impact of moose browsing on boreal-type forests of Isle Royale National Park. The American Midland Naturalist **95**:79-92.

Sokal, R.R., and Rohlf, F.J. 1995. Biometry. 3rd ed. W. H. Freeman and Company, New York, N.Y., U.S.A.

Suominen, O. 1999. Impact of cervid browsing and grazing on the terrestrial gastropod fauna in the boreal forests of Fennoscandia. Ecography 22:651-658.

Suominen, O., Danell, K. & Bergström, R. 1999. Moose, trees, and ground-living invertebrates: indirect interactions in Swedish pine forests. Oikos 84:215-226.

Stewart, G. H., and L. E. Burrows. 1989. The impact of white-tailed deer *Odocoileus virginianus* on regeneration in the coastal forests of Stewart Island, New Zealand. Biological Conservation 49:275-293.

Stockton, S. A., S. Allombert, A. J. Gaston, and J.-L. Martin. 2005. A natural experiment on the effects of high deer densities on the native flora of coastal temperate rain forests. Biological Conservation 126:118-128.

Stokstad, E. 2005. Ginseng threatened by Bambi's appetite. Science 307:827.

Stormer, F. A., and W. A. Bauer. 1980. Summer forage use by tame deer in northern Michigan. Journal of Wildlife Management 44:98-106.

Stroh, N., C. Balzinger, and J.-L. Martin. 2008. Deer prevent western redcedar (*Thuya plicata*) regeneration in old-growth forests of Haida Gwaii: Is there a potential for recovery? Forest Ecology and Management. 255:3973-3979.

Stromayer, K. A. K., and R. J. Warren. 1997. Are overabundant deer herds in the eastern United States creating alternate stable states in forest plant communities? Wildlife Society Bulletin 25:227-234.

Sternberg, L. 2001. Savanna-forest hysteresis in the tropics. Global Ecology and Biogeography 10:369-378.

Suding, K. N., S. L. Collins, L. Gough, C. Clark, E. E. Cleland, K. L. Gross, D. G. Milchunas, & S. Pennings. 2005. Functional- and abundance-based mechanisms explain diversity loss due to N fertilization. PNAS 102:4387-4392.

Thomas, L. J. L Laake, S. Strindberg, F. F. C. Marques, S. T. Buckland, D. L. Borchers, D. R. Anderson, K. P. Burnham, S. L. Hedley, J. H. Pollard, J. R. B. Bishop, and R. A. Marques. 2005. Distance 5.0. Release Beta 5. Research Unit for Wildlife Population Assessment, University of St. Andrews, St. Andrews, UK.

Tilghman, N. G. 1989. Impacts of white-tailed deer on forest regeneration in northwestern Pennsylvania. Journal of Wildlife Management 53:424-453.

Vila, B., T. Keller, and F. Guibal. 2001. Influence of browsing cessation on *Picea sitchensis* radial growth. Annals of Forest Science 58:853-859.

Vila, B., F. Torre, J. L. Martin, and F. Guibal. 2003. Response of young *Tsuga heterophylla* to deer browsing: developing tools to assess deer impact on forest dynamics. Trees-Structure and Function **17**:547-553.

Waller, D. M., W. S. Alverson, and S. Solheim. 1996. Local and regional factors influencing the regeneration of eastern hemlock. Regional conference on ecology and management of eastern hemlock, Iron Mountain, MI 73-90.

Waller, D. M., and W. S. Alverson. 1997. The white-tailed deer: a keystone herbivore. Wildlife Society Bulletin **25**:217-226.

Webster, C., M. A. Jenkins, and J. H. Rock. 2005. Long-term response of spring flora to chronic herbivory and deer exclusion in Great Smoky Mountains National Park, USA. Biological Conservation **125**:297-307.

Webster, C. R., M. A. Jenkins, and G. R. Parker. 2001. A field test of herbaceous plant indicators of deer browsing intensity in mesic hardwood forests of Indiana, USA. Natural Areas Journal **21**:149-158.

White, G. C. 1992. Do pellet counts index white-tailed deer numbers and population change?: a comment. Journal of Wildlife Management. **56**:611-612.

Whitlaw, H. A., and M. W. Lankester. 1994. The cooccurrence of moose, white-tailed deer, and *Parelaphostrongylus tenuis* in Ontario. Canadian Journal of Zoology-Revue Canadienne De Zoologie **72**:819-825.

Wiegmann, S. M., and D. M. Waller. 2006. Fifty years of change in northern upland forest understories: Identity and traits of "winner" and "loser" plant species. Biological Conservation **129**:109-123.

Wiegmann, S. M., and D. M. Waller. ms. Do deer drive long-term shifts in plant nutritional status? 50-year changes in the composition of Wisconsin forest understories. For Oecologia.

Williams, C. E., E. V. Mosbacher, and W. J. Moriarity. 2000. Use of turtlehead (*Chelone glabra*) and other herbaceous plants to assess intensity of deer browsing on Allegheny Plateau riparian forests, USA. Biological Conservation **92**:207-215.

Williams, N. S. G., J. W. Morgan, M. J. McDonnell, & M. A. McCarthy. 2005. Plant traits and local extinctions in natural grasslands along an urban-rural gradient. Journal of Ecology **93**:1203-1213.

Williams, T. M., J. A. Estes, D.F. Doak, and A. M. Springer. 2004. Killer appetites: assessing the role of predators in ecological communities. Ecology **85**:3373-3384.

Wisconsin DNR, 2005. Deer abundance records URL: http://dnr.wi.gov/org/land/wildlife/hunt/deer.

Woods, K. 2000. Dynamics in late-successional hemlock-hardwood forests over three decades. Ecology **81**:110-126.

NPS D-88, April 2009